Papercraft
Step-by-Step

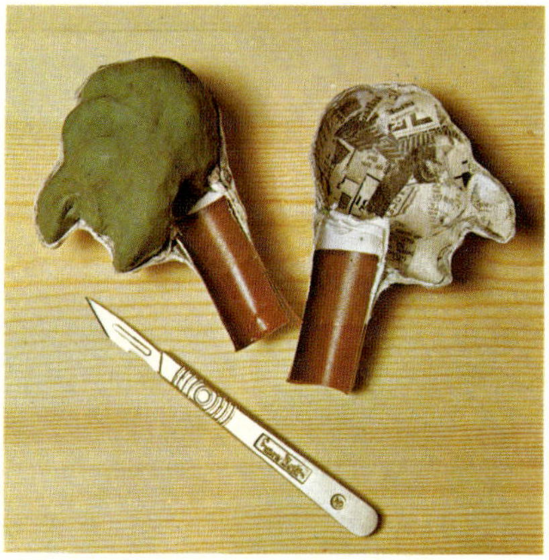

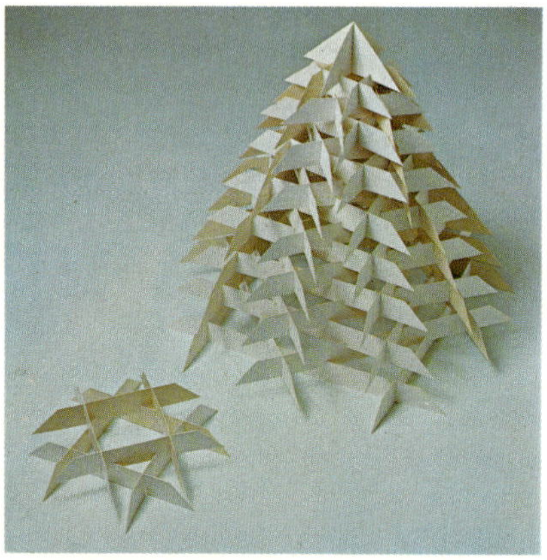

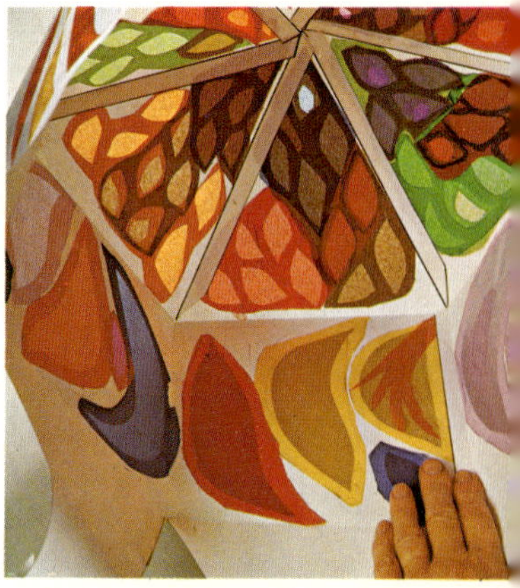

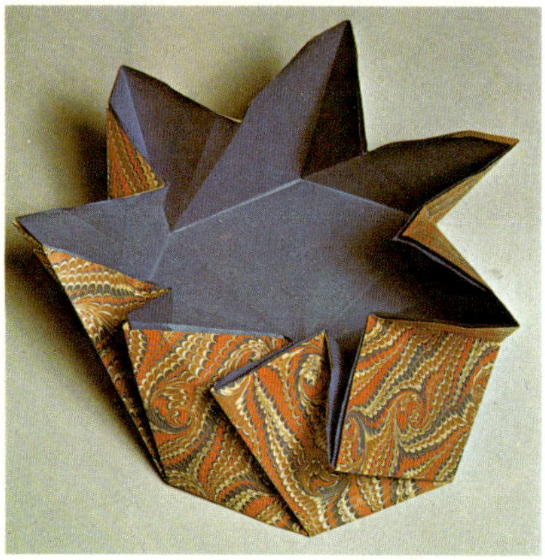

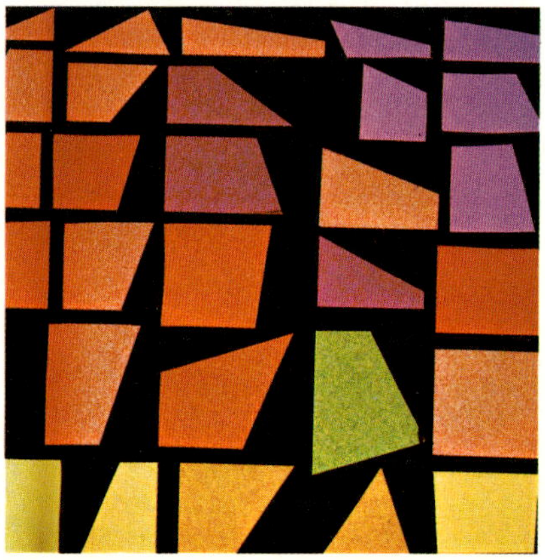

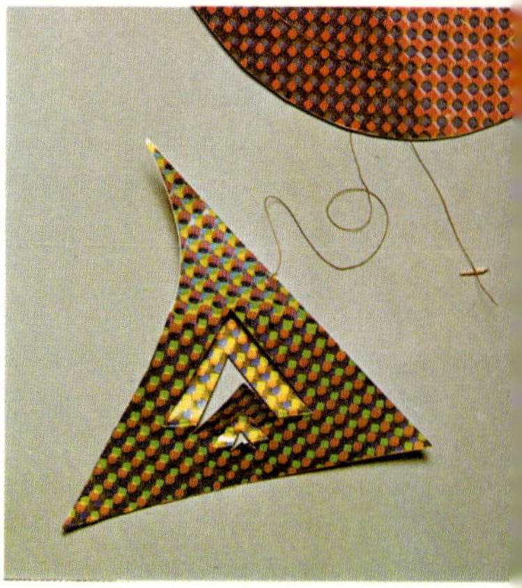

Papercraft

Step-by-Step

June Jackson

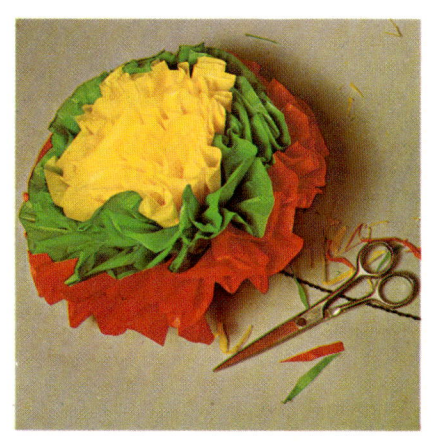

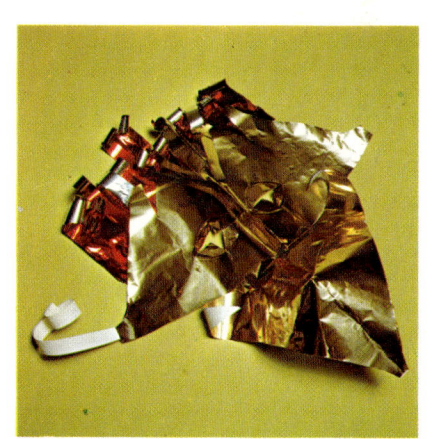

Collier Macmillan Canada, Ltd

Written by June Jackson
Pages 13–15, 29–38, 44–47
and 58–61 by Hannah Skipper

Photographs by Peter Kibbles

A Studio Vista book published by
Collier Macmillan Canada Ltd.
1125B Leslie Street,
Don Mills, Ontario M3C 2K2

Copyright © Studio Vista 1977
First Published in 1977

All rights reserved. No part of this book may be
reproduced or transmitted in any form or by any
means, electronic or mechanical, including photocopying,
recording or by any information storage or retrieval system
without permission in writing from the Publisher.

ISBN 0.02.973180.1   Papercraft

Set in VIP Times Roman by Amos Typesetters, Spa Road, Hockley, Essex, England.

Printed in Great Britain by Sackville Press Billericay Limited
Billericay, Essex, England

Contents

Introduction to Papercraft	7
Basic Techniques	8
Surface Decoration	11
Windmills and Spinning Tops	13
Mobiles	16
Translucent Light Patterns	18
Translucent Lampshades	20
Pleated Lampshades	22
Pleated Blind	24
Collage and Photomontage	26
Straw Ball	29
Paper Flowers	33
Garlands	36
Containers	39
Paper Cookery	42
Locking Shapes	44
Boxed Boxes	46
Masks	48
Magic Theatre	50
Puppet Theatre	55
Papier Mâché	58
Kaleidoscope	62

6

Introduction to Papercraft

Some of the paper and equipment you will need to make the things in this book.
Paper Across the top, left to right; printed marbled paper; red Ingres paper; hand blocked Venetian paper; four marbled papers; three Japanese papers, yellow orange and blue; hand-made straw paper; hand-made Japanese lace paper. Across centre, left to right; red and violet hand-made papers; Japanese textured paper; coloured acetates; red metallic paper; mirror foil; selection of coloured tissues. In the foreground; black card; white kent paper.

Drawing materials, instruments and adhesives Left; small guillotine; steel T-square; steel ruler; steel straight-edge; wood dowelling. Centre; tin of emulsion paint with brush; tin of rubber solution and spreader; adhesive tapes; black fibre marker. On the white paper, left to right; adjustable set square; gouache designers colours; black poster paint; plasticine; craft knife and blades; Stanley knife; paint brushes; compass with cutting blade; drawing pins; scissors; pencils; wooden spatula; set of coloured fibre pens.

As paper is one of the cheapest materials available you can start on many of the projects in this book with the minimum outlay. Although there are many beautiful and expensive hand-made papers (see opposite page) to buy once you have learnt the basic techniques, you can begin by experimenting with old newspapers, magazines and cardboard boxes and achieve attractive results. The simplest projects in this book require only pieces of paper and your fingers, but a basic set of tools should include an accurate ruler for measuring (if this is made of steel it will also double up as a straight edge for cutting); an assortment of sharp pencils, both hard and soft, for marking, measuring and designing; sharp craft knives with spare blades; adhesives, a dry glue is invariably the best (water glues tend to distort the papers and cause the colours to run when used with tissue papers), adhesive tapes, double-sided adhesive and a rubber solution. You also will need a good flat surface to work on and a separate surface on which to cut, such as hardboard or a piece of thick cardboard. It is a good idea to visit your local art supplies shop and look at the different weights, textures and colours of paper and card: feel the difference between foil and newspapers, between four-sheet card and sixteen-sheet card, so that you know what is available when you come to tackle the projects.

Each of the following projects introduces you to a particular technique so that by the time you have worked through the book you should have grasped all of the basic skills involving cutting, folding, pleating, papier mâché, and collage, and be able to go on and design your own projects. You will also begin to understand how to use daylight and artificial light for the best results when making the lampshades, the window screen, the magic theatre and the shadow puppets and eventually you should have made many attractive presents for your family and friends — a kaleidoscope, paper flowers, glove puppets, gift boxes and containers, and many more.

Basic Techniques

You will need:
Sheets of cartridge-paper
Metallic paper
Newspaper
Tissue paper
A ruler
A spatula, or back of a knife
Scissors
Scalpel, or craft knife
A hard pencil
About 1 m (1 yd) of thin string
Drawing pins
Glue, for paper

Flat paper
A piece of flat paper is inanimate. It is also a fertile field containing possibilities of creating visually exciting objects, both decorative and practical. The first and most important way to work with a material is to understand its characteristics, respect them, and exploit them. Really effective use can be made of paper by understanding its basic structure, and also being aware of the importance of light, whether from without or within, as an element in designing with it.
The surface structure of a flat piece of paper can be changed by folding, bending, cutting shapes within it, while still remaining

1 Pull the paper firmly from a flat surface holding a ruler on edge across it.

2 Roll a piece of paper in a ball and squeeze it, allow it to spring back, making its own shape.

3 Fold a square of paper diagonally, turn it over and fold sideways, creating a star.

4 Fold the paper to the centre, crease firmly, and continue folding to the fold.

two-dimensional; or by cutting and shaping to create a three-dimensional form.

Curving
Paper can be curved into a single bend, or pulled on alternate sides to create a wave effect; for this method, use a firm paper such as cartridge-paper or kent. Curve it by pulling it firmly over the edge of a table, or by holding a ruler across and pulling it through (1). The paper will remain in this form, its body structure now being altered. To increase the light patterns reflected from the surface, spray it with a paper varnish.

Creasing
The effect of light reflecting from a creased surface will vary with different weights of paper; creasing is arbitrary, but the controlling factor is the fibre content of the paper. Try this with different kinds of paper—tissue paper, a firmer paper such as cartridge or layout paper, and a brittle, metallic paper (2) and experiment with different light sources.

Folding and pleating
A more controlled effect is gained by folding and pleating, and for this use a firm paper such as layout- or cartridge-paper. By folding in different directions, and on both sides of the paper, star shapes and other patterns can be made (3). Where large pieces of paper are being folded or pleated, score gently along the inside line of the fold, with the spatula, or back of a knife. To make the folds permanent and sharp, run the spatula along the crease. Pleating consists of first folding the paper at regular intervals in one direction only. Intervals can be measured, or alternatively, fold the paper in half, then

5 Turn paper over, place peaks of outer folds together, and crease, making a valley fold.

6 Make a hole and pull the pieces out from the paper, leaving an opening with a rough, uneven edge.

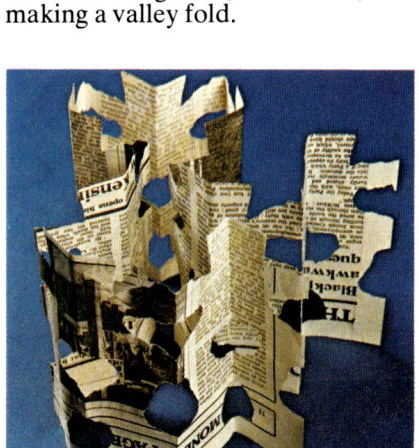

7 Patterns made by folding and tearing, using a thin paper, in this example, newspaper.

8 Cut shapes in a flat piece of paper, pull up, folding and pressing at different angles.

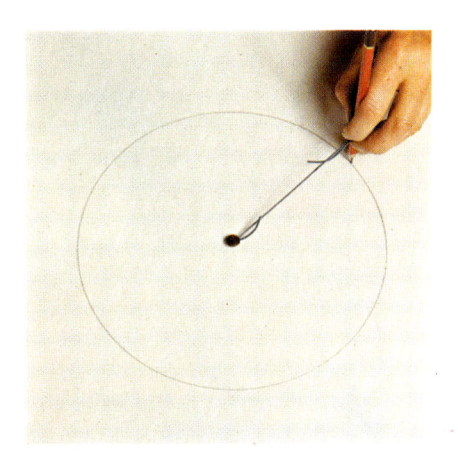

9 Attach string to a drawing pin, tie to a pencil at end of the radius, and draw a circle.

10 Press folds and margins with a spatula to give a sharp figure. Glue the edges together.

the half in half, (4), and continue until the intervals are twice the required width. Reverse the paper, (5), and make the 'valley' folds. Keep the edges absolutely in line to produce regular even folds.

Cutting and tearing
To alter the face of the paper, you can cut, tear, and pierce it, and the changes effected in any one method will be infinitely variable with changes in the light source. Tear shapes from the paper (6) not severing them but bending and curling them by pulling over the shaft of a pencil, using your thumb as a support at the back. This gives new textures to the surface; holes, pieces at angles from the face, and shadows cast by the light. Torn shapes give arbitrary and unexpected effects (7); cut shapes can be controlled, and shapes can be cut within shapes, folding in different directions (8); holes punched through, or pierced with a gimlet, will filter light on to the paper.

Three-dimensional forms
The simplest three-dimensional form, a hanging mobile, is made from a single cut in a piece of paper; it takes the form of a spring, and can be circular or angular. The knife is taken from a point within the edge of the paper, and a continuous line cut through to the centre in a spiral not allowing the line to touch itself at any point, as this would result in two or more minispirals. The falling coil of paper can then be suspended from its centre point to twirl in space.

The cube, the cylinder and the cone
Of the geometric solids, the simplest to make is the cylinder. It is a flat piece of paper, rolled round, and the edges glued together. A cone is made from a portion of a circle; half, or three-quarters, giving more or less open cones. A large circle can be drawn using a drawing pin a piece of thin string, and a pencil; the size of the circle being limited only by the length of the string, (9). Hold the pencil firmly, and maintain a constant angle, preferably upright. A circle or any part of it can be drawn like this. Mark out a segment, cut the figure out, and glue the two straight edges together.

The cube is made by drawing a cross with six square faces, the upright being formed of four squares, the arms a square at each side of the second square, and with margins for glueing (10).

These simple progressions from the flat piece of paper are elements which form the basis for many of the projects that follow.

Surface Decoration

RUBBINGS

You will need:
Fine grained rag paper, white or coloured
Heelball, or wax crayon
Masking-tape
Collection of leaves, wood, coins and other items for rubbing

Making a rubbing produces a facsimile on the paper of the image on the surface. The surface to be rubbed has to have markings either in relief, standing out from it (1), or intaglio, cut into it (2). There are many textures that are suitable for rubbing — natural forms, leaves, wood-grain, grasses; and man-made forms, lace, wire mesh, coins (3); as well as stone carvings and brass engravings.

Fix the paper in place over the texture, using masking tape at the corners; and rub the crayon evenly over the surface. Feel where the edges are, to avoid spilling over, and occasionally check for any detail that has been missed. The crayon leaves its mark where it is in contact with the surface. If it is intaglio, the design is revealed as a white line (4). The relief image emerges as a

1 A stone boss in a garden wall. This is an example of high relief and would need a heavy paper.

2 A number cut into a wood surface. The wood itself will give an attractive texture.

3 Feathers, coins and other textures that will give interesting rubbings, relief and intaglio.

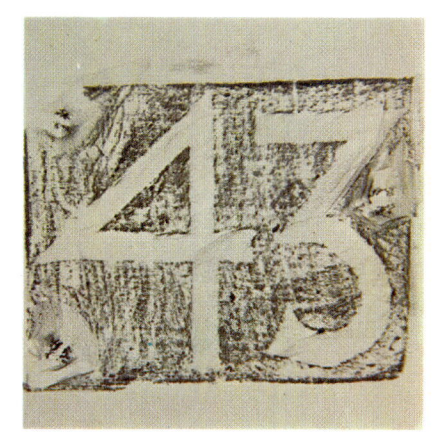

4 Rubbing of the engraved number. The image is negative, that is, the colour of the paper.

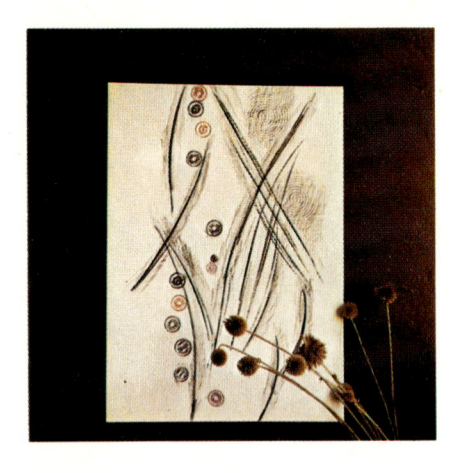

5 Rubbing made over textures. Feathers and coins give a positive image, the colour of the crayon.

6 Coloured gummed paper cut into small pieces. If the paper is not gummed use a dry adhesive.

7 Working the design; grouping and distributing the chosen colours to create an abstract design.

dark line, (5). Brass rubbings are made in this way; but first get permission from the vicar, and second, dust the surface carefully to remove any grit, before and after working.

MOSAICS

You will need:
Strong cover paper for the base
Gummed coloured papers
Scissors

A mosaic is a picture built up of many small square shapes of different colours, stuck on to a base. There are the mosaics made from ceramic and glass, cemented on to a wall or floor surface, notably, early Roman and Christian examples in Ravenna. Paper mosaic uses similar techniques, but being more flexible, paper can be overlapped and the shapes varied. A design can be worked out on the paper first, or alternatively, cut a number of pieces and place them on the paper before sticking them down (6) allowing ideas to form as you see the shapes on paper. Work on one small area at a time (7) sticking down when you are satisfied with the design.

12

Windmills and Spinning Tops

WINDMILLS

You will need:
2 sheets coloured sticky paper
1 plastic straw
1 stick
1 pin
Scissors
Ruler
Pencil
Glue
Paint brush
A jar of water

The best sort of paper to use for a windmill is shiny and sticky-backed. Use two contrasting colours together. To stick the squares together, use the water very sparingly, painting it onto the back of one square, and carefully placing the other square down onto it. To get the edges well matched up it is better to cut the squares too large, stick them together, and then trim them down to size. Make up the windmill as shown (2-3) then attach it to the stick (4). The piece of straw between the stick and the windmill acts as a washer and allows the windmill to turn freely whilst the other piece stops the pin wearing through the paper.

1 Cut two pieces of paper 150 mm (6 in) square and stick together, using water very sparingly.

2 Draw diagonal lines and measure 70 mm (2¾ in) in from each corner. Mark alternate corners with an 'X'.

3 Cut along the lines and stick the corners marked 'X' into the centre without folding them.

4 Cut pieces of plastic straw and assemble with the pin. Tap the pin firmly into the stick.

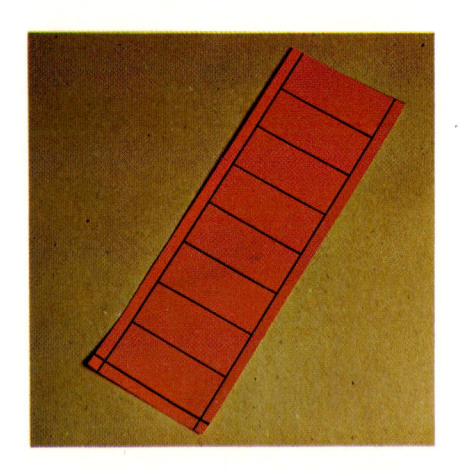

5 Cut and stick two rectangles 330 mm (12½ in) × 110 mm (4½ in). Draw margins and dividing lines.

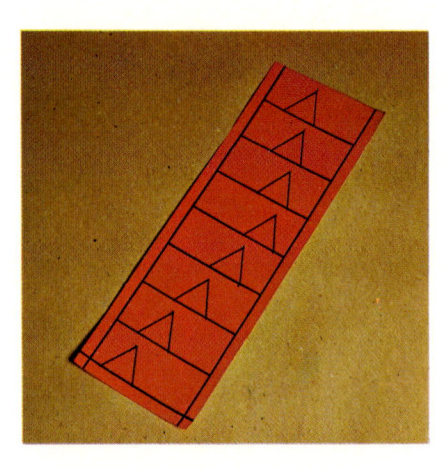

6 Measure and draw out the triangles. Carefully cut out the points of the triangles with a craft knife.

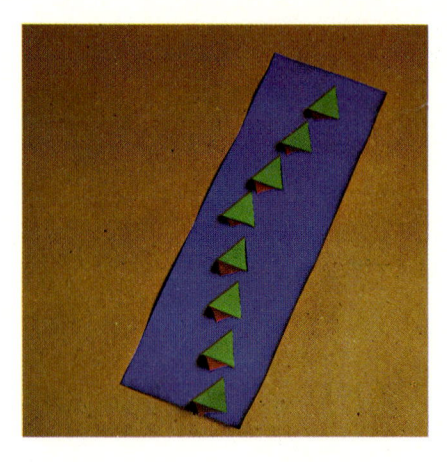

7 Turn back the points of the triangles and stick the third colour, green, onto the back.

8 Form the rectangle into a cylinder and line with stiff card sticking it firmly into place.

9 Make up the three pieces of dowel into the spindle using pins. Snip round the cartridge-paper discs.

10 Join the lid and base to the spindle and stick the assembled wheel in place inside the cylinder.

WINDMILL CYLINDERS

You will need:
3 sheets coloured sticky paper
1 sheet of card
1 sheet of cartridge-paper
Ruler, craft knife, glue
Thin dowelling, 2 pins
Wire cutters

Draw three margins 10 mm (½ in) wide on one short side and on both long sides of the rectangles (5). Divide the remaining 320 mm (12 in) × 90 mm (3½ in) into eight sections 40 mm (1½ in) wide. Starting with the small margin line, measure 10 mm (½ in), 25 mm (1 in), and 40 mm (1½ in) down. The middle point should be extended at 90° to the straight line and marked off at 30 mm (1¼ in). Join the top and bottom mark to the extended point to form the triangle. Repeat measurements to the next line 10 mm (½ in) further down, and continue in this way until you have done the fifth line. Go back up by 10 mm (½ in.) until you reach the eighth line. Cut triangles and stick on third colour (7). Make a cylinder of card, put inside cylinder to stiffen. Cut dowelling 100 mm (4 in), 25 mm (1 in) and 40 mm (1½ in), and stick pins in the small pieces. Make top and base by cutting circles 100 mm (4 in) in card, and circles 125 mm (5 in) in cartridge, and sticking together (9). Snip the edges and stick the pins through the middle of the circles. Cut pin heads off, and stick the ends into the long piece of dowelling. Tap gently with a hammer until only a small amount of pin is showing. Spread glue on the snipped edges and position carefully in the cylinder. Allow to dry and stick to base.

14

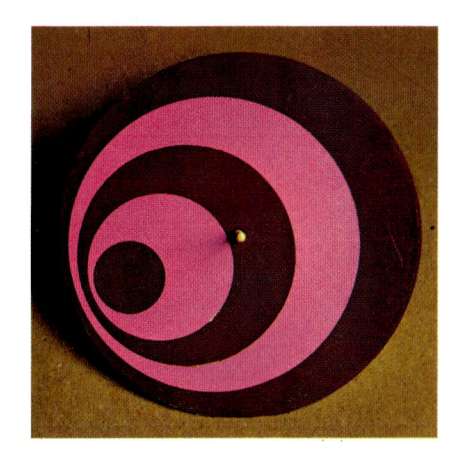

11 Cut a circle out of stiff card and draw your own optical design in strongly contrasting colours.

12 Cut a star in the centre of the circle with a craft knife and push the dowelling through it.

13 Cut a long tapering piece of paper, glue it on one side and wind it round the dowelling.

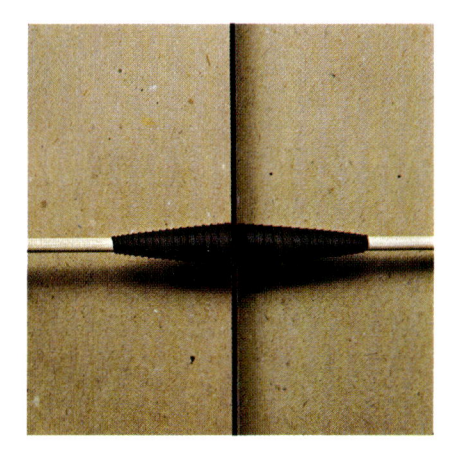

14 Wedge up firmly against each side of the disc and glue into place. Taper spinning end of dowel.

SPINNING TOPS

You will need:
A sheet of stiff card
Wood dowelling
Glue
Craft knife
A compass
Coloured paper or pens

Experiment with the effect of optical illusion on the disc, either using contrasting colour or lines of stark black on a light background. If you are not satisfied with the result, stick a different pattern on top.

15

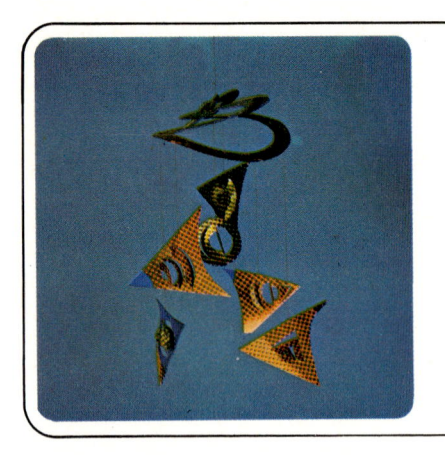

Mobiles

Mobiles are suspended shapes that rely on currents of air to give them movement. They should be light in weight, and have a surface, or surfaces, to present against the air, like the sails of a windmill.

FLAT MOBILES

You will need:
Thin card
Cartridge-paper
Patterned papers
Craft knife
Glue (rubber solution)
Strong thread

These mobiles are cut from paper with different patterns on each side; the patterns can be painted on, or patterned papers can be stuck together (1). A rubber solution is best, because it is a dry method; the paper will lie flat, and any excess gum can be rolled off. The central mobile is cut from thin card to support the weight of the smaller paper mobiles. It starts as a large circle, with incomplete concentric circles cut within it (2). Cut the smaller mobiles from cartridge-paper, also patterned (3) and with centres cut and folded within

1 Place gummed sheets together; smooth firmly with closed fists, from the centre out, in all directions.

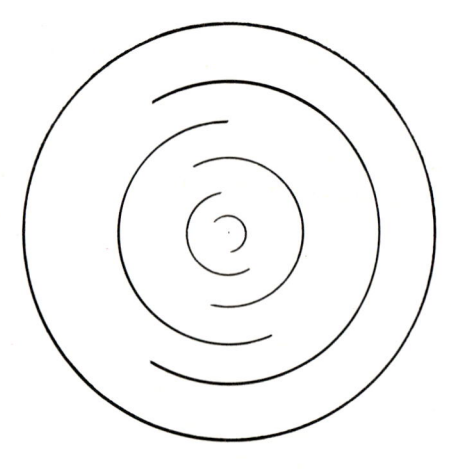

2 Draw out part circles, as shown here, and cut them with a craft knife or cutting compass.

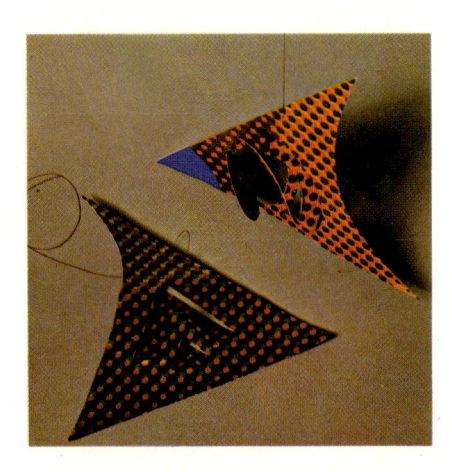

3 Small mobiles have cut centres, round and triangular, giving them an independent rotation.

4 Suspend main mobile by a thread through its centre. Make holes on the circle to take minor mobiles.

them, giving them 'fins' for independent movement. Suspend the main mobile (4) to assess hanging points; the additional weight of the smaller mobiles will change its shape by opening up the circles. Attach the small mobiles to the parent mobile, and adjust length of hang. The mobile pictured here also has one suspended from its centre.

SOLID MOBILES

You will need:
A sheet of cartridge-paper
Poster paint
Paint brush
Pencil
Ruler
Craft knife

These three-dimensional mobiles are designed as teasers. The intention is to make the mobile in one solid, and pattern it to disguise its actual shape, giving it an ambiguous appearance. This is the principle of camouflage. As some animals and insects take on the visual pattern of their background — leaves, twigs, sun and shade splotches, to render them invisible to their enemies, here, round shapes can appear to have corners, straight-edged shapes to curve and bend. Draw out the shape for the three-dimensional form (6) and paint or glue the pattern onto the flat shape, visualising the effect across the joining edges. Let the design go over the edges to be cut, to avoid unpainted bits showing at the joins. Picture (7) shows how this works on the cube. For other shapes, make a small model first, and number the joining areas. Before making up the mobile decide the point of suspension and attach the thread. The mobiles can be hung individually or in one long string

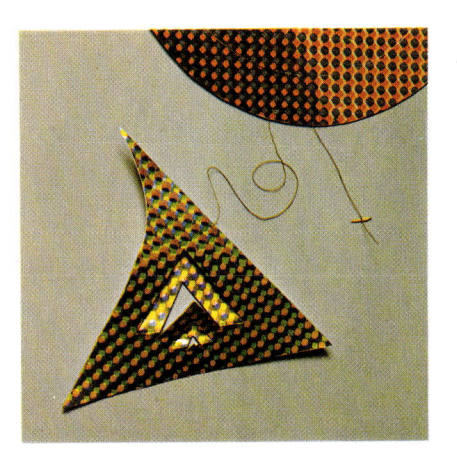

5 Suspend minor mobiles from the main mobile. Experiment with hanging from different points.

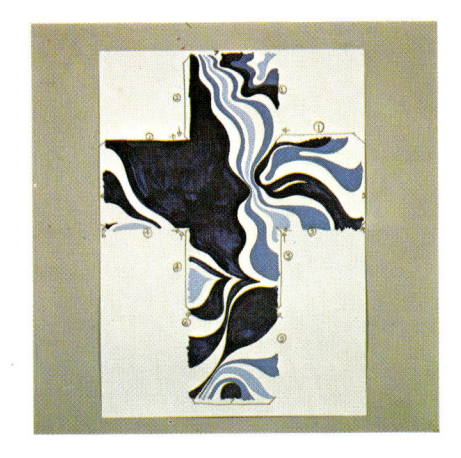

6 Draw out the cube; number the sides that will join, and note the direction of join.

7 Make up the cube by applying glue to the flaps, and sticking them on the inside.

Translucent Light Patterns

Light used externally, directed onto relief designs on white paper, makes a variety of different patterns. The patterns are created by shadows cast from the shapes, the gaps from which the shapes have been removed, and the shapes themselves. The patterns will change dramatically by altering the direction of the light. Light used internally, or from behind, will give luminosity, especially when contrasted against a dark opaque ground. Coloured tissue paper, coloured acetate, and other very thin papers used in this way, give the effect of stained glass windows.

Light is an integral part of this form of papercraft; its effectiveness depends on light shining through the translucent inserts. If your light source is daylight, as the light changes, you will get luminosity in duller weather, to brilliant shafts of coloured light, reflecting on other surfaces in the room, and moving as the sun moves. Artificial light on the other hand, is a constant, unchanging source, which will diffuse the light. Artificial light will alter the appearance of the colour; tungsten light is yellow, and acts as a filter, causing consider-

1 Lay the pieces of tissue paper against the light to see their effect both by daylight and electric light.

2 Draw the design in a light coloured chalk on the reverse side of the paper and fill in the shapes.

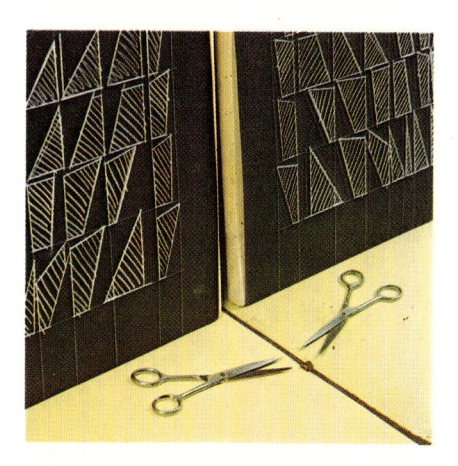

3 Look at the reflection of the design to check its positive image and make any alterations.

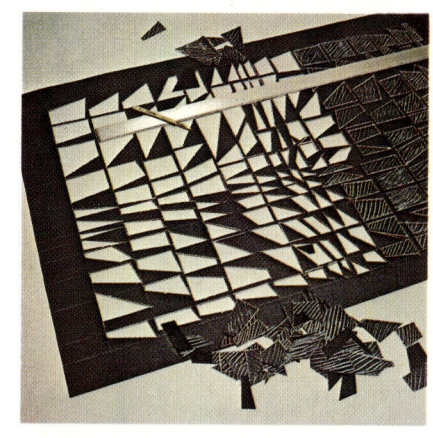

4 With a sharp craft knife carefully cut away the areas to be covered by tissue, leaving retaining walls.

able change in the colour. Try the tissues against different light sources to assess the effect on colour changes (1).

WINDOW DECORATION

You will need:
Heavy dark opaque paper, the size of the area to be covered
Sheets of coloured tissue paper
Paper-glue
Craft knife
Scissors
Straight edge
Light coloured chalk

The dark paper should be strong enough to remain rigid such as cover paper or paper similar in weight to a heavy cartridge. Cut it to the shape required to fit the window. Working on the wrong side of the paper, or what will eventually be the back of the design, draw out a pattern from which holes will be cut or torn, leaving a border in proportion 1:24 all round, for strength (2). As the completed design will be in reverse, refer to its mirror image (3) before cutting. Designs can be very controlled, using a carefully measured grid with geometric cut-outs. Try using tracings from plants, leaves, or other organic shapes, or arbitrary, chance shapes cut or torn from the paper. When the design is completed remove the areas which will supply the 'windows', (4). Several layers of tissue can be overlaid, to increase intensities of colour, or to give changes of colour within one area. Tissue can be glued to tissue, and holes can be removed from some tissues. Experiment with the tissue before finally glueing it down. When it is complete and dry, fix it to the window, using double-sided adhesive or a plastic adhesive.

5 Place the tissue over the design covering several windows at once and draw the shape to be cut.

6 Glue round all the edges of the windows to be covered. Cut out the tissue shape and stick down.

Translucent Lampshades

You will need:
A sheet of white or coloured paper, cartridge weight
Coloured tissue paper
Glue
Pencil
Ruler
Scalpel or craft knife
Scissors
500 mm (20 in) thin nylon cord

Paper burns and electric light bulbs produce heat; but by allowing air to circulate, and leaving sufficient space around the bulb, the lamp shade will not present a fire risk. The space to allow will be in ratio to the power of the bulb; to a 40w bulb, allow a diameter of about 300 mm (12 in), and a clearance at all points from the bulb of at least 80 mm (3 in). The paper for the shade should be light in colour, unless you want a dimly-lit, mysterious effect; good for atmosphere but poor for reading by. Consider this, and try the paper against a light before making a decision.

The lotus-shaped lampshade has tissue inserts and, as with the window decoration, you will need to assess the effect of light through the papers; ideally do this when it is dark and all light source

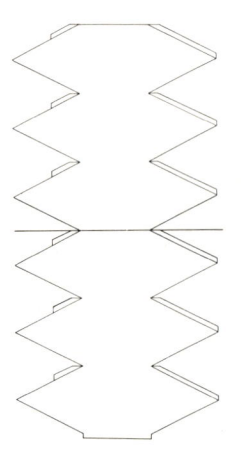

1 Draw the flat shape for the lampshade leaving narrow bands for glueing as shown here.

2 Cut out the pattern shapes and glue on the inside of the shade. Turn over and check colour density.

3 Curl the tops of the triangles on the top band using a round pencil or piece of smooth dowel.

4 Fold the body of the lamp then glue the triangles leaving the 'petals' free at the top.

is from artificial light. The paper for the shade, whether white or coloured, should have the weight and fibrous quality of a good cartridge to give curve to the 'petals'. To make the basic shape lay the paper with its longest measurement horizontally. This will form the circumference of the shade. Divide the paper horizontally into three bands, each measuring 130 mm (5 in), and divide the paper vertically into six equal parts, after leaving a 10 mm (½ in) band at the end for glueing (1). To make the triangles in the top and bottom bands, find the centre in each division, and draw a line from the point on the outer line of the band. On one side of each triangle leave a glue band. The top triangles on the shade form the petals, and on these the band stops 60 mm (2½ in) from the main body.

The waste areas can now be cut away. Make the tissue inserts, following the directions for the window decoration, working on the inside of the shade. Cut the tissue neatly round the edge of the holes after sticking as they will create shadows on the shade. A lampshade is also seen in daylight, so the design must satisfy two requirements; as a light-diffusing object affecting the room, and as a sculptural object, relating to the room. When working out the design (2) visualise the shade as both images; lit from within, projecting coloured light; and as a solid object in an external light source. When the tissue inserts are dry, curl the petals (3) and fold the sections ready for assembly (4). Make up the shade (5). Sew a fine nylon cord through two facing petals first sticking a piece of paper on the inside to reinforce (6) and attach securely to flex.

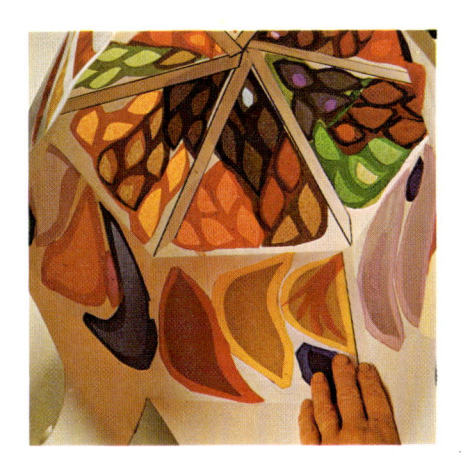

5 Join the body round on the inside by overlapping the margin and glueing down.

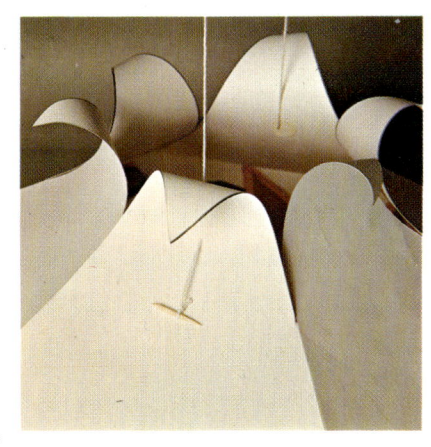

6 Pass the cord through two of the petals which are opposite each other and secure with toothpicks.

Pleated Lampshades

The simplest pleated lampshade is a long rectangular piece of paper, evenly pleated, the two ends joined to form a continuous cylinder. By passing a cord through the pleats at each end, the cylinder can be modified to form a cone varying the diameters top and bottom.

HANGING LAMPSHADE

You will need:
3 sheets of Japanese textured paper, or similar
Transparent adhesive tape
Thin cord
Big lampshade ring, with inner ring for lamp socket
Small wire ring for base of cone

For the measurements of the paper, allow twice the width of the widest diameter; in this shade, the depth is 600 mm × 3 m (24 in × 3 yd). The shade is attached to the frame by over-sewing the cord to the base ring. It is not always possible to get frames exactly to size and adaptations have to be made (4). Prepare the pleating in the usual way. When the shade is joined in a complete cylinder (3) it will need some support while the frame is set in place (5).

1 Score the paper with a spatula before folding to create sharp, even pleats.

2 Pierce holes through paper in the centre of pleats 30 mm (1¼ in) from edge. Thread cord through.

3 Join shade by butting edges together. Stick on inside with transparent adhesive tape.

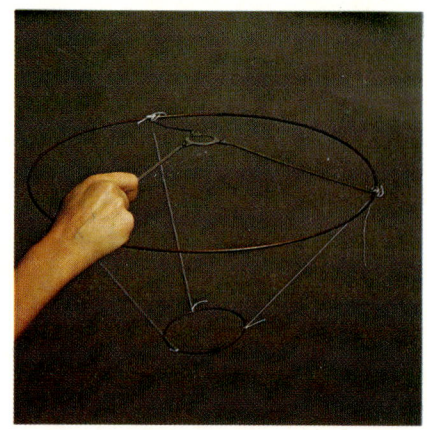

4 Join the two rings together with cord as shown, checking the diameters against the lampshade.

22

5 Set frame inside the shade keeping it upright. Oversew the base ring to the cord in base of the shade.

6 Make a small fold in the centre, and also folds down the outer halves a little over half way as shown.

7 Fold in half and prepare pleats in the usual way giving extra pressure over double folded areas.

8 Pull out and open gently from the middle keeping the pleats as even as possible.

9 Pull out the side folds. These will fold under, to the base, and in, to the top.

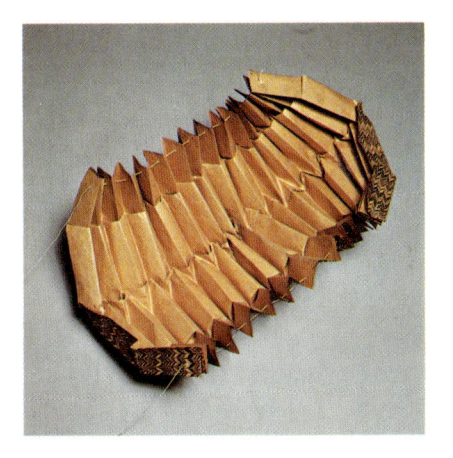

10 Thread cord through top and bottom of shade and join up to make a cylinder, adjusting cords to fit.

FREE-STANDING LAMPSHADE

You will need:
2 sheets of marbled paper
Thin cord
Wire ring for base
Transparent adhesive tape

To make more complex forms, the pleating and folding is combined. By folding the paper before pleating (6) the shape will be broken into more planes, with alternating pleat patterns. When the shade is completed fix the wire ring in the base to keep it even.

Pleated Blind

You will need:
Strong paper, cartridge, or book linen, one third longer than the length of the window and as wide as the window, or the width less 60 mm (2 in) if it is going inside the window frame
2 pieces of ply-wood, 4 mm (⅛ in) thick, one the length of the width of the paper, one longer by 60 mm (2 in)
2 'L' brackets
Screws for fixing blind
3 screw eyes
Blind cord, 6 times the length of the window
Wooden acorn for ends of cord
Strong wood glue
Drill
'S' hook to wind cord on
Screws to fix
Wood-seal or varnish

Paper for the blind should be chosen after deciding how much light you want it to exclude. A pale coloured paper will dim and diffuse the light, but will allow shadow silhouettes to show through; a deep-coloured or black paper will obscure all vision on the other side, and effectively darken a room. Patterns can be painted or pasted onto dark or light paper before pleating, to

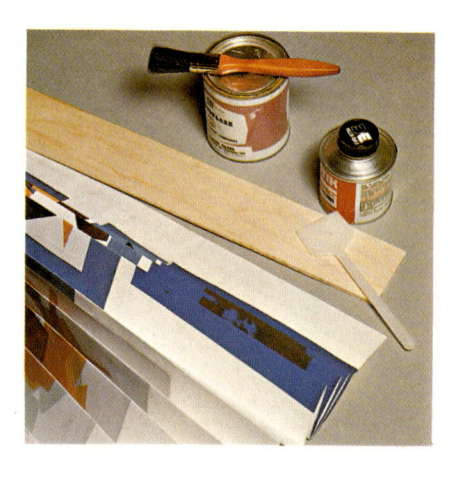

1 Seal wood on one side, glue unsealed side to top and bottom pleats.

2 Drill holes right through wood and pleats at each side, and through over-hang for cord.

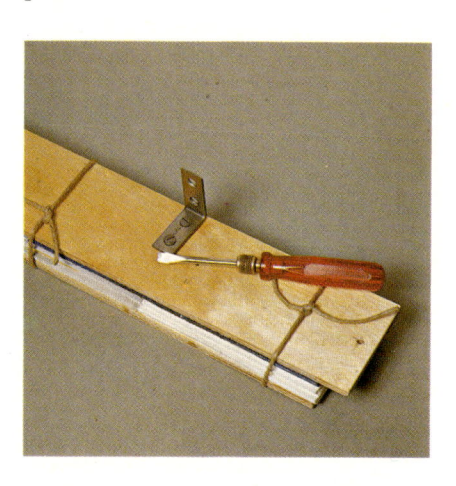

3 Screw 'L' brackets on back of top strip, for fixing outside window frame.

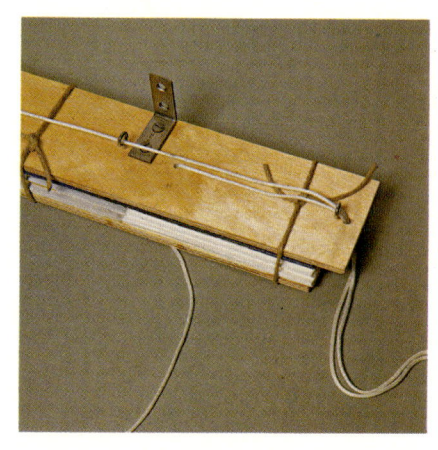

4 Fix screw eyes on inside of brackets and before exit hole; thread cord through holes and eyelets.

5 Even up the cord and shorten if necessary allowing for full extension. Attach the acorn.

make a feature of the blind when the room is lit. Measure the paper to the width of the window, allow for the 60 mm (2 in) on one side for the pull cord. In measuring the length of the blind allow approximately a third extra, as the blind remains in shallow pleats when fully extended. Thus on a drop of 1.7 m (5 ft), 2.2 m (7 ft) should be sufficient. Work on a large flat surface where you can lay the paper out, and start by folding the paper in half, and follow directions for pleating on page 9, aiming at a finished pleat of about 40 mm (1¼ in). Keep the folds as even as possible, otherwise the result may be a spiral blind; interesting but not very practical. The top wood strip is now glued to the descending pleat on the right side of the paper (1) leaving an overlap of wood on one side. Use a strong bonding glue, and follow directions fully allowing time to dry. The bottom strip is glued to the last pleat on the under side of the paper. The holes are now drilled to take the cord (2). Fold the blind into a tight concertina and clamp or tie it down, place a piece of waste wood underneath before drilling. Make a mark on the top strip 100 mm (4 in) in from each edge of the paper, that will be 100 mm (4 in) plus the overlap, and centred in the strip (2). Make a further mark on the overlap, centred between the end of the paper and the end of the strip. Right or left is unimportant, but it is the side that will operate the blind. If the blind is to fit on the outside of the frame, fix the 'L' brackets, (3). If it is to inset in frame, fit the brackets to the extreme ends of the strip, facing sideways. Fold the cord in half, and thread one end, starting at top of non-operative side, coming up to meet the other half (4) passing through screw eyes fitted to one side of the holes, to give easy running. Take both ends of the cord through the overlap, and with blind extended, even up the cord (5) and fit the acorn. Fit the blind into position in the window, leaving a gap above the top strip to allow free movement of the cord. Adjust and shorten the cord if necessary, and fix the 'S' hook at a convenient point on the window frame to hold the cord.

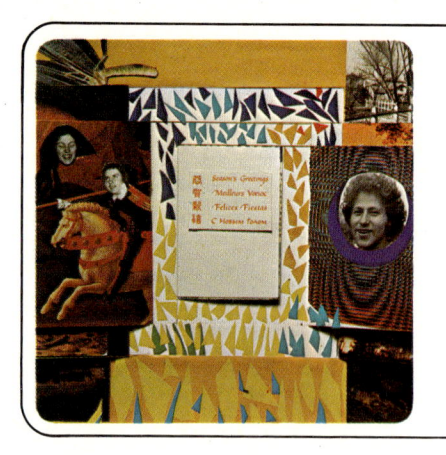

Collage and Photomontage

The invention of the photograph produced a popular art form of a sort only previously achieved by the invention of the printing press. By the end of the nineteenth century facsimile images of friends and relatives were available to everybody, and making one's own photographs became an equally widespread and popular occupation. The photograph album held almost as prominent a position as the family bible. A new form of decoration emerged replacing the embroidered hanging and the petit point fire-screen — the collage covered draught-screen. These screens were covered with a mixture of family photographs, printed decorations like flower patterns, coloured papers, prints and photographs from popular magazines of the day, picture post-cards, wrapping papers, shells and dried flowers. Collage is a form of picture-making where the images and shapes are cut out of other pictures, pieces of paper, fabrics and any bits of interesting texture. These are stuck down on a base creating a new composition. Photo-montage is concerned with putting together photographic images, and re-photographing

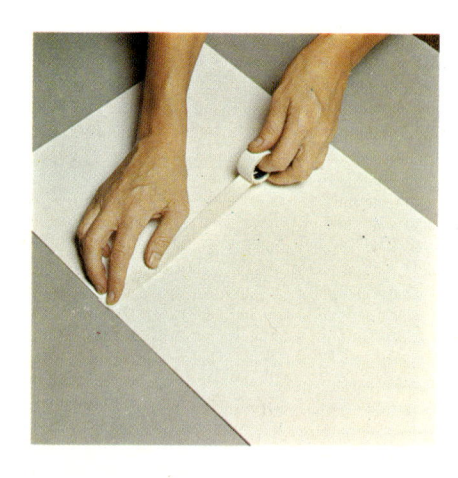

1 Score card on outside fold with scalpel, re-inforce inner fold with adhesive tape.

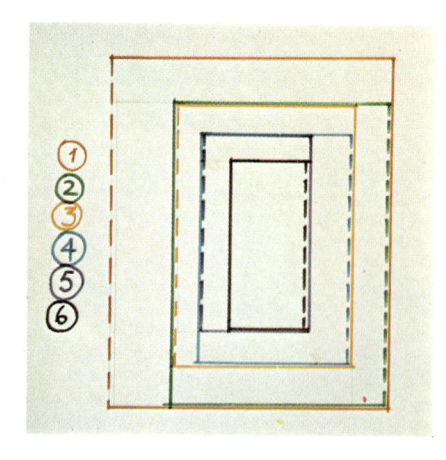

2 Make a plan of the opening windows. The hinge side is indicated by a dotted line.

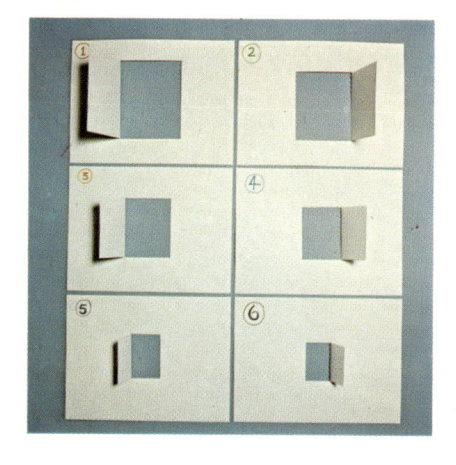

3 Number each sheet separately, and check its alternating opening pattern.

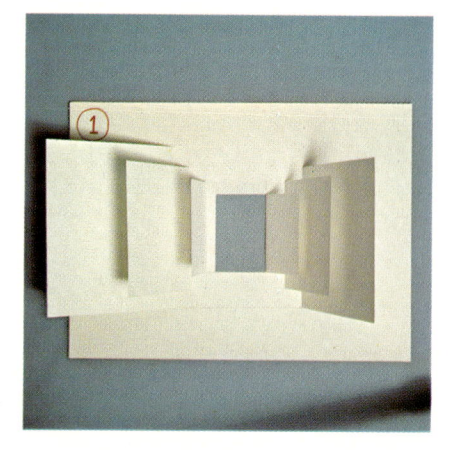

4 Place sheets over one another in order, and note frame surrounds for collage.

26

them, sticking unrelated pieces together to create new and imaginative compositions, not unlike the seaside photographer's lifesize picture with a hole for the client to stick his head through.

GREETINGS CARD

You will need:
Thin mounting card, 800 × 300 mm (32 × 12 in)
7 sheets of cartridge paper, 400 × 300 mm (16 × 12 in)
Photographs of family or friends
Magazines, newspapers, general ephemera for collage
Scalpel, or craft knife
Scissors
Glue (rubber solution)
Adhesive tape
Ruler
Coloured fibre pens, or paint
Paint brush

The device of this greetings card takes the form of a series of autobiographies; each member of the family, or contributing group making a montage from things associated with activities, ideas and personal preferences. The layout of the card gives each person a facing page for a written message. In the family card, the diminishing sizes relate to the diminishing ages of each member; an alternative arrangement can be worked out, giving all members an equivalent space.

The basic structure is a sheet of card the ends of which fold back to form wings to make the card free standing. The wings fold flat to the back of the card for posting, and they need reinforcing with adhesive tape on the inside fold to prevent them from cracking and breaking off (1). The size of the card should not exceed the maximum accepted by the Post Office for letter post. The total size of this card before folding is 800 ×

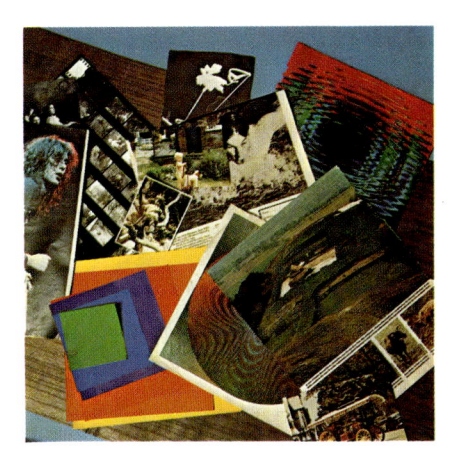

5 Assorted patterns, textured papers, coloured gummed papers, and photographs to select from.

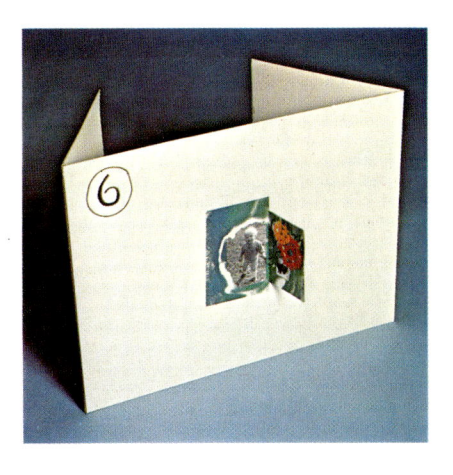

6 Make first image on base, stick sheet 6 in place, and continue on inside of opening.

7 Place 5 over 6, make image on inside of window, and continue pattern round frame area.

8 Fix last sheet in place, forming front cover. Make sure all the windows operate easily.

300 mm (32 × 12 in). Measure in 200 mm (8 in) from each end, score and bend to make wings (1). Cut seven sheets of drawing paper 300 × 400 (12 × 16 in). Take one sheet and draw out the window plan (2). Window 1, red, is 125 mm (5 in) from each side, 50 mm (2 in) from the top and 65 mm (2½ in) from the bottom with the hinge on the left. Window 2, green, is 25 mm (1 in) down from first window, 30 mm (1¼ in) in to the left from 1 with the hinge on the right. Window 3, orange, is 20 mm (¾ in) from the bottom of 2, with the hinge on the left. Window 4, blue, is 12 mm (½ in) in from the left of 3 and from the top, with the hinge on the right. Window 5, violet, is 20 mm (¾ in) from the right of 4 and from the bottom, with the hinge on the left. Window 6, black, is 12 mm (½ in) from the left and top of five, with the hinge on the right. Trace one window plan onto each sheet of paper, and cut (3). When they are assembled they will look like step 4, with windows open.

Make a collection of suitable photographs and other material (5). Starting with the base arrange parts of the collage and try to

27

visualise the total effect before sticking down. The pieces on the lower sheets can always spread over the edges to be covered by subsequent sheets. Glue sheet 6 in place and carry on the design on the inside of the window (6). Glue 5 down over 6 and continue patterning the spaces around the message area. This card is designed to carry six contributing members, one of whom is too young to write his own message. Apart from 6, the message area is on the back of each preceding window. The top sheet, 1, is the cover. It presents the closed card, and should be a composite picture conveying a total message, rather like headlines in a newspaper; or a simple design which is compatible to the whole effect. In either case, the first opening is conceived as part of the design, possibly taking the form of a door (8), inviting you to go in. Each person now writes his message on the closed window of the sheet below their image, and the card is complete.

VARIATIONS

A simpler form of window card can be made, using a base card, and a single overlay sheet; an advent calender has yuletide images which are revealed day by day, until all images are presented. Stick the images on to the base card and lay a sheet of tracing paper over to mark the position of the windows. Transfer the marks to the cover paper, and cut the window flaps as before. Open the flaps to avoid sticking them down, and glue the cover paper to the base card. Close the flaps and design the cover as before, to present a coherent picture with the images beneath.

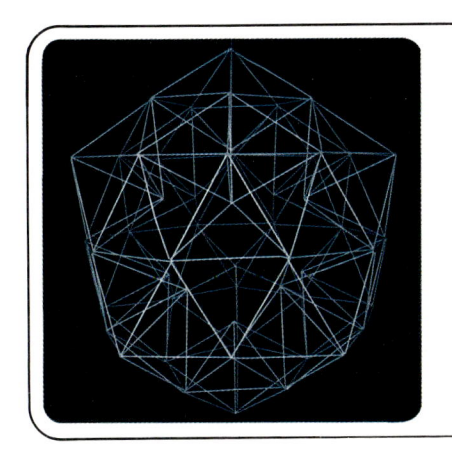

Straw Ball

You will need:
200 paper drinking straws
1 darning needle
2 reels white button thread
2 hooks
Scissors

Plain paper straws are not always easy to find; and they tend to be sold in small packs, usually the coloured candy-striped kind. These are uneconomical, and do not look very good when they are finished. Good newsagents, however, will order boxes of white paper straws. It is possible to use plastic drinking straws and these are more readily available, but they have several disadvantages. Firstly, because of the way in which they are made they are slightly curved making the end result less impressive, and secondly, they have a tendency to split down the length if the thread is pulled too tight. The disadvantages with paper straws are that they are weaker than plastic straws and if handled too roughly they will bruise or fracture. If a straw is bruised or in any way damaged, it must be replaced. Any deviations in the pattern of the finished ball will be very conspicuous, its visual effect rely-

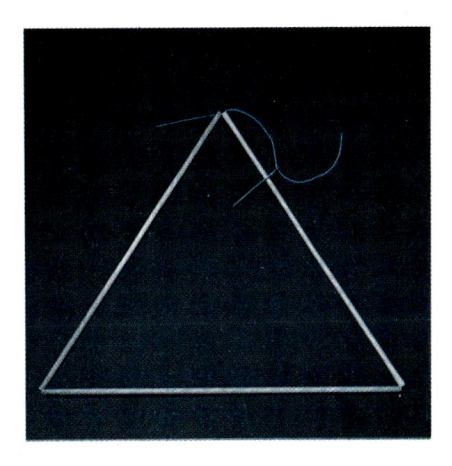

1 Thread on 3 straws and tie off the end to form a triangle. Leave the thread attached.

2 Using 8 straws, thread on 2 at a time to make 5 triangles. Repeat (1) and (2) 11 times to make 12 forms.

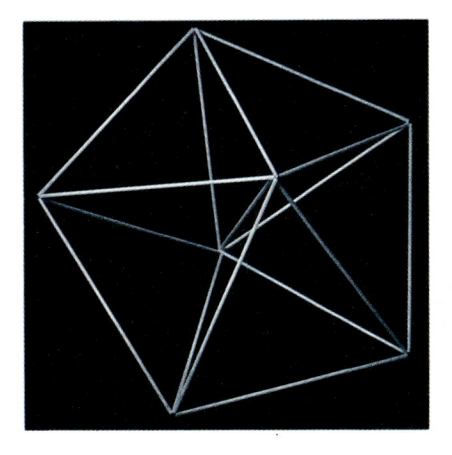

3 Take one form, and add 5 straws to it from point to point, to make a rigid form.

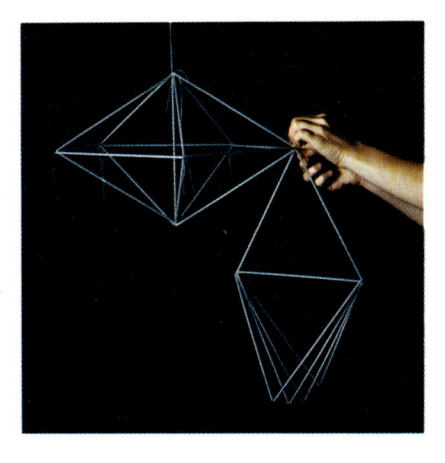

4 Hang the rigid form at working height, then tie one of the remaining forms to a corner.

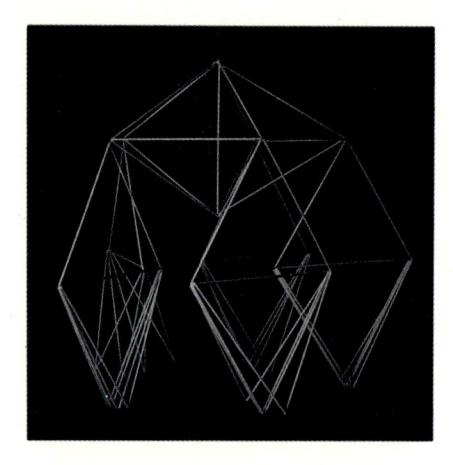

5 Tie the other 4 forms to the remaining 4 corners. This forms the base for the first half.

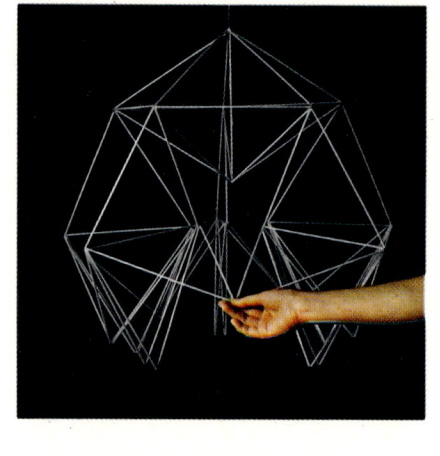

6 Take 1 triangle from hanging form, tie it to the nearest triangle on the next. Repeat all round.

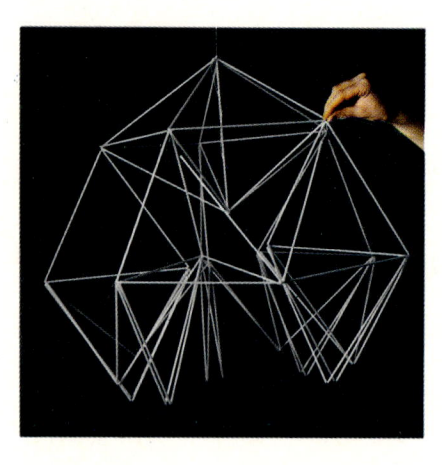

7 Add 2 straws, 1 from one corner to the points just tied, the next, from there to the next corner.

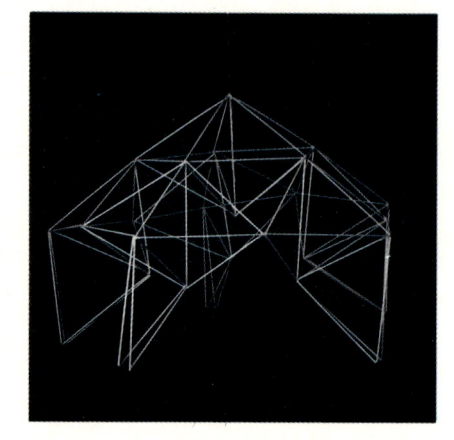

8 Repeat (7) on other 4 sides, to leave you with a larger solid structure with ten triangles hanging down.

ing on its geometric precision.

Using as long a thread as you can manage thread on three straws and tie off the end, to form a triangle (1). Do not cut the thread; put on the next two straws beginning the next stage of the structure. When the structure is complete, as in (2), repeat eleven times, to end up with twelve structures. Put six of these to one side, and concentrate on one half of the ball. Take one of the six forms and add five straws to it to make a rigid structure, as in (3). Hang this at a working height (4), either standing or sitting, and tie the remaining five forms as shown, from each corner (5). Each structure has four triangles hanging down from it. Tie the triangles together, as in (6), and begin the next building process. From now on, the process becomes more difficult to follow. Using another ten straws, two at a time, tie the end of the thread to a corner where you first hung one of the limp forms, and thread on a straw (7). Loop the thread around the point made by the two triangles tied together. Pull it reasonably taut, and thread on another straw. This straw is joined to the next corner around. Without breaking the thread, join the next straw and continue as before. When you have used up all ten straws you should be back at the point at which you began. Having reached figure (8), there are now two triangles hanging down from each group. Using fifteen straws, three at a time, tie thread to the point exactly between the hanging triangles of one group, and the next. Thread on a straw, and join it to the nearest hanging triangle on the left, thread on another straw, and join that horizontally to the nearest triangle on the right. Finally, thread on the third straw and tie it to the point at which you began. Repeat the process on the remaining four spaces, to make (10) which is a complete half ball. If possible, leave it hanging where it is, and begin making the other half. This should progress more easily than the first half.

The construction of a straw ball will take about a day from start to finish. Before starting on the ball, make sure you have sufficient space; particularly for the hanging of the two halves. A very important factor to account for, is the size of the finished ball. If you are using white paper drinking straws, about 250 mm (10 in) long, the finished straw ball will measure nearly 1250 mm (4 ft) across. Alternatively, plastic straws, which measure 210 mm (8¼ in), make a more manageable ball, the finished size being under 930 mm (3 ft). Construct the ball, therefore, in the room in which it will be hung, or conversely, make up the two halves and take them to their final destination before tying them together. When you have completed the construction of the two halves, decide how you want to finish the ball off, before joining them

9 Add 3 straws. From tie-on point to hanging triangle, from there to next triangle, and back to start.

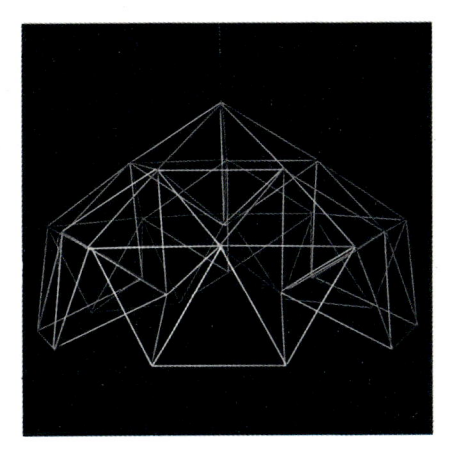

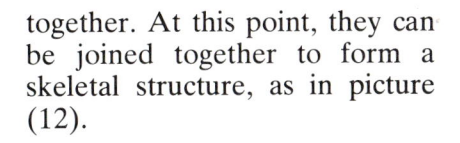

10 Repeat on remaining 4 sides to complete half a ball. Repeat steps 3 to 10 to make the other half.

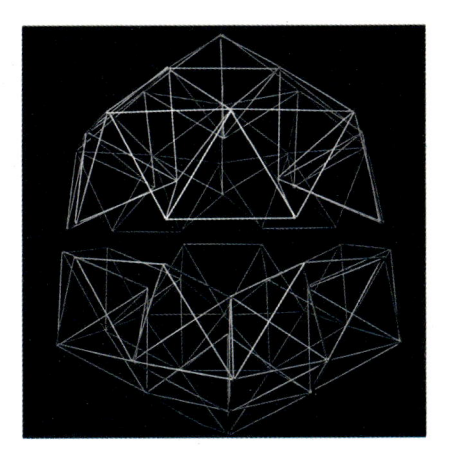

11 Tie the two halves together to make a ball, and trim off all the hanging threads. Hang it up.

together. At this point, they can be joined together to form a skeletal structure, as in picture (12).

COVERED STRAW BALL

You will need:
80 squares coloured tissue paper
Scissors
Glue

If you wish to cover the outer skin of the ball with tissue paper, this can be done with the halves tied together. Cut out at least 80 triangles, slightly bigger than the triangle formed by three straws tied together. This allows an overlap for glueing. Then working from the top down, stick on the triangles, very carefully.

INNER COVERED BALL

You will need:
80 squares coloured tissue paper
Scissors
Glue

If you wish to cover the inside skin of the straw ball, this must be done in two halves. In order to ensure that no harm comes to the straws during glueing I would

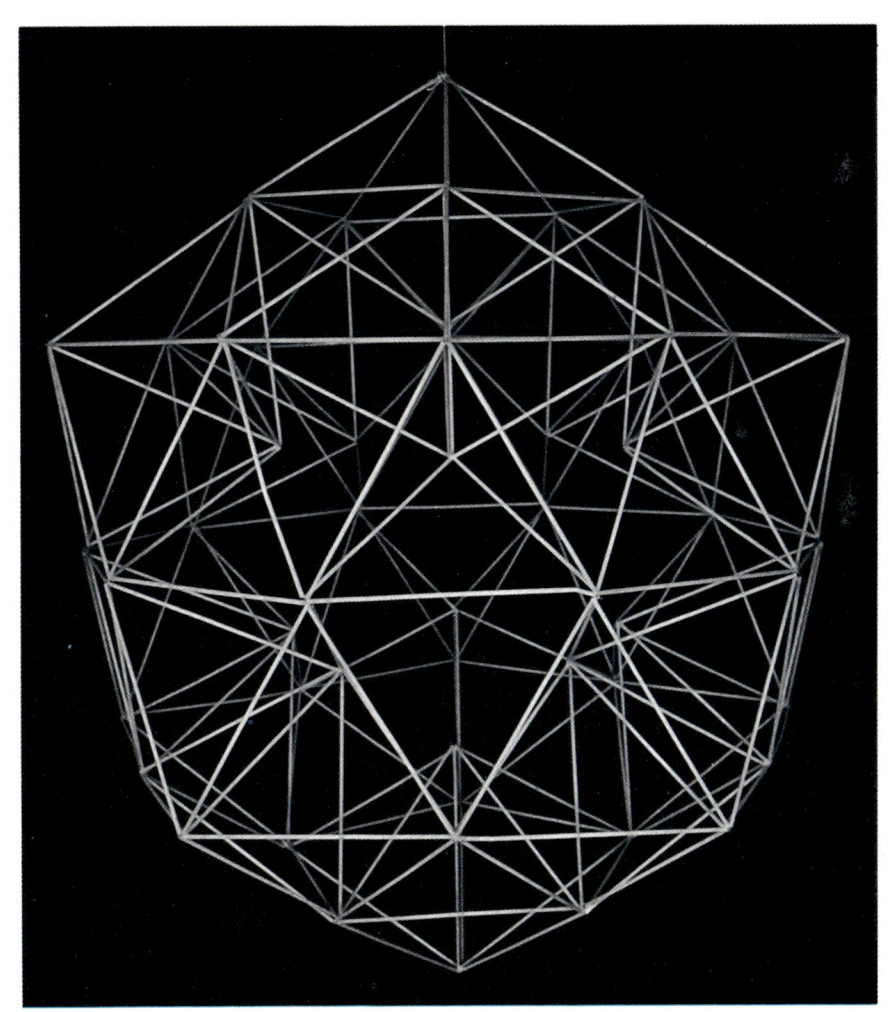

12 The completed ball. Get someone to help you hold the lower half of the ball whilst you tie it to the hanging half. Make sure that you assemble the two halves in the room where you want the ball to hang.

31

recommend working with the half balls on a work surface, rather than hanging. First select your colour or colours of tissue paper, and then cut out 80 triangles, using a triangle of straws as your template. Lie the half ball down on its side with the inside facing. The best sort of glue to use is a tube glue with a thin nozzle so that you can draw a line round the three sides quickly and evenly. Try also to find a glue that dries quickly, this stops the triangles peeling away while you are working. Work from the middle outwards, and try and revolve the half ball so that the triangles you are sticking are face down onto the work surface. Not all the triangles can be face down, but there is less risk of the straws being damaged if you work in this way. When both halves are covered, tie them together, and hang.

If the ball is to be used with a light suspended inside, leave a triangle uncovered at the top for the flex and lamp socket to pass through, and attach to the flex by a thin cord, ensuring that the bulb has a good clearance all round (for recommended clearance, see translucent light project on page 20).

Other variations of the straw ball can be devised once you have mastered the basic building techniques. Make smaller balls by cutting the straws in half or spray the straws in a variety of bright colours so that each of the twelve sections can be made in its own colour.

Paper Flowers

TISSUE PAPER FLOWERS

You will need:
Coloured tissue paper
Scissors
Green plastic-coated wire
Wire cutters
Small weight

Tissue paper flowers are a simple and effective decoration, used either to bring colour and variety into a daily situation, or massed and scattered on festive occasions. The variations that can be achieved are almost endless; real flowers can be interpreted in colour mixtures, size or shape. For reference, seed catalogues are very helpful as they have almost every garden flower, and a few more besides. The pictures are all in colour, and they are very easy to analyse.

Select the colours to be used, and lay them out with the colour chosen for the middle of the flower on top (1). Weight down the end of the tissue and fold in 25 mm (1 in) folds. Bind the middle with the wire, and twist all the way down. Treating the paper very gently, peel up the layers one by one, all the way round. When the final layer has been peeled up,

1 Cut a length of wire 460 mm (18 in) long, and fold in half. Cut tissue into strips.

2 Line up the paper carefully, weight down the end and fold in 25 mm (1 in) folds.

3 Fasten the middle with the wire and twist the two lengths together to form the stem.

4 Pull up the layers of tissue one layer at a time, all the way round.

33

trim it, to tidy any uneven ends.

To make a carnation-type flower, first select the colours, then snip along the top and bottom edges; this gives a frayed effect to the flower. To create a mottled effect, take pieces of tissue the same width, but only about 50 mm (2 in) to 100 mm (4 in) long, and slip them at random in between the layers of tissue and treat in exactly the same way as the previous flower.

PETAL FLOWERS

You will need:
Coloured paper
Scissors
Ruler
Glue
Card

The paper used to make these flowers is a hand-made Japanese paper, coloured all the way through, as opposed to only surface coloured paper.

Make up the template 75 × 35 mm (3 × 1½ in) from a hard card, draw round it and cut out the fifteen petals (6). Divide the petals into three groups of 5, cut all three groups 25 mm (1 in) in at one end. Cut the other ends of the petals; 12 mm (½ in) in the first group, 18 mm (¾ in) in the second, and 25 mm (1 in) in the third (7). Glue the first cuts in an overlap, to make the petals stand up; glue the other cuts to make the petals bend the other way (8). Take the group with the 12 mm (½ in) cuts first, and stick them together with the small cuts uppermost, to form the inside of the flower. Turn it upside down, stick the next five on in the spaces between the first group, finally stick the petals with the 25 mm (1 in) cuts at both ends on the very outside. Finish off with a spray in the middle (9).

5 When all the layers are pulled up, trim all round the edges.

7 Divide into three groups of five. Measure and make cuts in each group as shown.

CONE PETAL FLOWERS

You will need:
Coloured papers
Ruler
Scissors
Glue

This flower is very simple to make but rather time consuming in preparing the 50 cones. To make the cones, wrap the squares (10) round the index finger, and glue down one side. Build up the flower (11). This finished structure is very strong, therefore it can be made larger and be used as

6 Make up the template out of stiff card. Cut out fifteen petals using the template.

8 Stick all the cuts to make the petal shapes, join the first five together as shown.

an ornamental container for pencils or paintbrushes.

Right: Paper flowers are cheap to make and easily replaceable, allowing for changes of colour scheme and changes in mood or season. The Japanese papers are more expensive and less fragile both in texture and colour. They come in a more subtle range of colours, closer to those of Nature.

9 Stick the rest of the petals together and make a centre-piece to finish it off.

10 Cut out fifty 50 mm (2 in) squares and make into cones. Stick 16 onto a disc of card to form the base.

11 Stick 14 on top for the next layer, then 12, then 8, then finally 3 for the middle.

Garlands

You will need:
Coloured tissue paper
A sheet of card
Scissors
Ruler

When drawing the templates (1) take plenty of measurements to ensure that one link will fit through the next (3). Select the colours of paper you are going to use, and fold. For the round shaped chain, fold the paper in half, and half again, the other two need only to be folded once. Place the template on the paper with arrows on the folds (2), and draw round them. Cut them out.

Plain paper can be used, as an alternative to tissue paper, particularly if there are children about, who would enjoy drawing patterns on it. But if you use tissue paper by only using two colours, a third colour is formed by the overlap. Another advantage is that as it is so thin, more links can be cut simultaneously. As tissue paper is rather fragile, the safest way to construct the garlands is to start the chain, then hang it on the wall and continue working on it. When it is finished hang it up completely to avoid it getting damaged. When the round-

1 Measure carefully, draw and cut out the templates making sure that links will fit together.

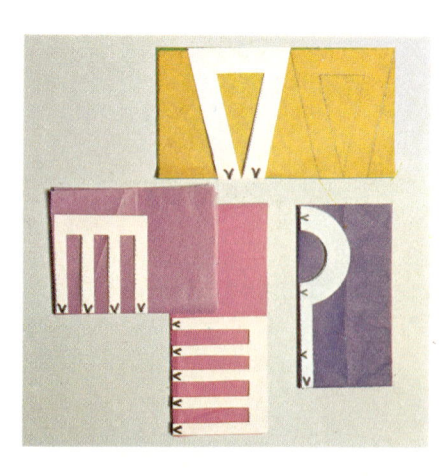

2 Lay the templates on the paper with the folds where the arrows indicate. Draw and cut out.

3 Link shapes together. For the forked shape garland, thread one through the side of the next.

4 Select the nine colours and cut into eight squares each. Divide into eight groups of nine colours.

shaped garland is made, a large number of discs are left over. These can also be used, as follows. Using a needle and cotton, thread on one disc then thread 10 mm (½ in) of straw. Continue, threading alternative colours and straws, until you have used all the discs up. There may well be other left-over pieces of tissue that can also be used; the making of the tissue ball which follows leaves a ready-made chain of a useful length.

TISSUE BALL

You will need:
9 sheets of coloured tissue
1 sheet of cartridge-paper
1 sheet of card
Scissors
Ruler
Glue
Tape

Cut each sheet of tissue into eight pieces and divide all the paper up into nine groups of eight colours (4). Make a plan from a sheet of paper 280 × 250 mm (11 × 10 in) and draw parallel lines down it 25 mm (1 in) apart (5). Mark every other line with an 'X', top and bottom. Cut out 50 strips of paper 25 × 225 mm (1 × 9 in), lay the first sheet of tissue on the plan, 12 mm (½ in) in from the first line. Using the ruler, draw thin lines of glue along each line marked (6) then place a strip of card between each line of glue. Lay the next sheet of tissue on top of that and glue along the unmarked lines (7). Place the strips down as before and continue until all nine colours are used up. Leave to dry then remove the protective strips of paper. Repeat the entire process another seven times to use up all the sheets of tissue. Stick the eight piles of paper together (9) making sure that the lines of glue

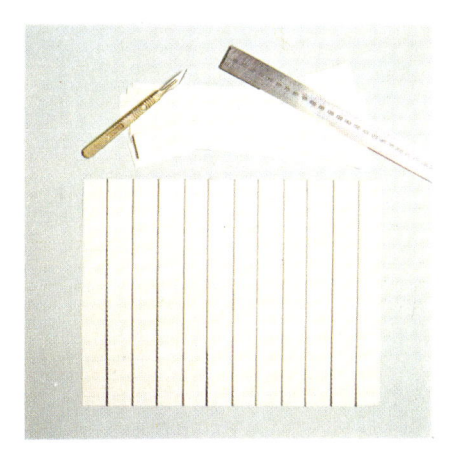

5 Make up the plan and mark every other line with an 'X'. Cut out the strips.

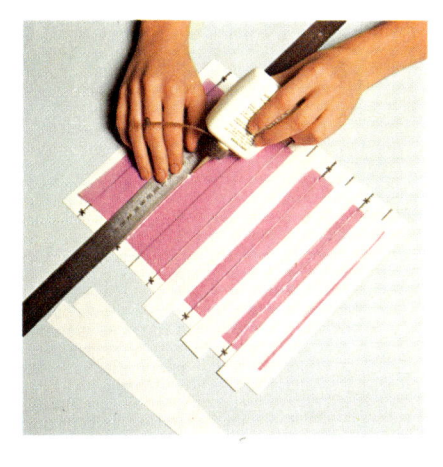

6 Glue along the lines marked 'X' and put the strips down in between the glue lines.

7 Glue along the un-marked lines and mask off between the lines of glue as before.

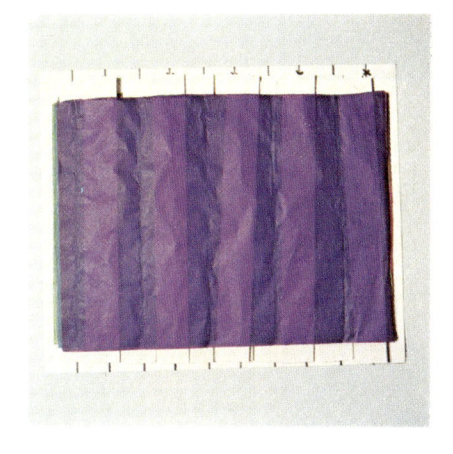

8 Continue alternate lines of glue until all 9 colours are stuck. Leave to dry before removing paper strips.

9 Glue the 8 piles together putting strips in the layers that are to be stuck.

10 Stick card to top and bottom of the pile and open out to make sure that none are stuck wrongly.

37

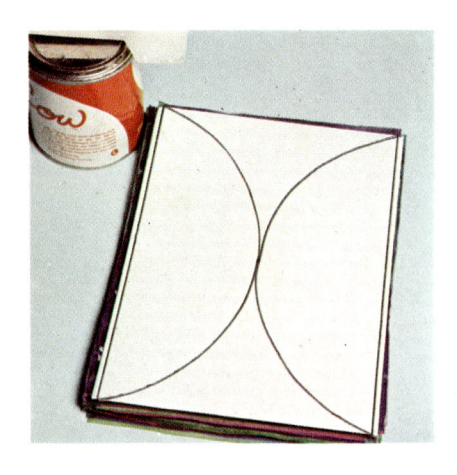

11 Mark out the two arcs putting the axes on the long edge, not parallel to the glue lines.

12 Cut out and stick the spine with strong tape, open out and clip with a paper-clip.

on the top of one pile are in the same place as the lines of glue on the bottom of the pile above. Stick a sheet of card on the bottom and top of the pile, then holding the top piece of card, drop the rest down to make sure that none of the sheets have stuck in the wrong place (10). It was necessary to use the strips of paper as no glue could be found that did not seep through one layer of paper and stick it to the next.

The pieces left over after the two balls are cut out can be used as garlands. See below.

Containers

Containers made of paper can be very complex but the simplest are often the most effective. One of the most common paper wrappers is the cone. Take a square of paper and with a dextrous roll of the hand (1) and a twist to the bottom the cone is secure. Flowers can be placed on the flat paper and the cone wrapped around them.

The Japanese form of folded packet uses no glue and relies entirely on folding and locking to maintain its shape. The paper used should be firm and once creased into folds should spring back into shape. Marbled papers and patterned papers with the weight and fibre of a good cartridge-paper should work well.

THE OCTAGON

You will need:
Two contrasting squares of paper

More permanent containers are made by following a pattern of folds. The size of the completed octagon will be half the size of the original square, its measurements therefore can be calculated around the intended contents.

1 Set square diagonally, pattern outside, and fold in a spiral. Twist bottom to secure.

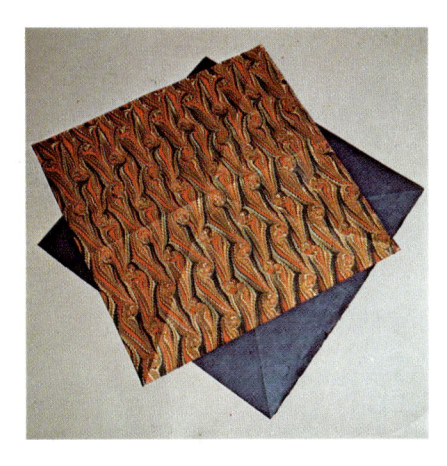

2 The octagon starts from a square of paper, a second square of the same size is used as a lining.

3 Fold paper across the square from side to side, and from top to bottom.

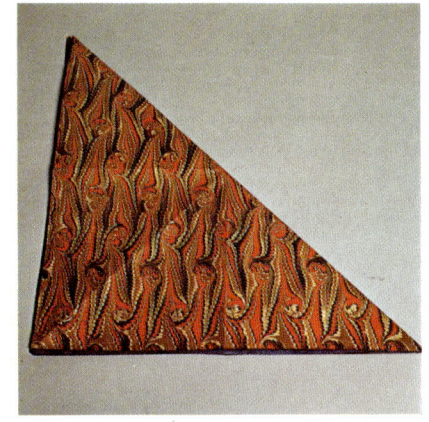

4 Fold the square on the diagonal, corner to corner, both ways, forming a star shape.

39

5 Measure from the centre to make fold lines the same length, cutting the square to form an octagon.

6 With the inside face upward, fold each flat side to the centre, crease well at the edge.

7 Fold the segments to the centre, following the same direction round the eight sides.

8 Press firmly in place. The paper will spring back into place after opening.

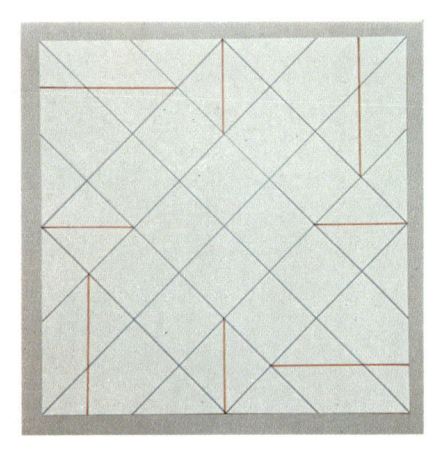

9 Blue lines fold with the inside of the paper facing, red lines fold from the outside.

10 Stand sides up from the base, fold back rectangles, make top by folding diagonally to centre.

The paper used here is a marbled paper and is patterned on one side only and for contrast a Japanese coloured paper is used as a lining (2). The two sides are placed with their insides facing each other and are folded throughout as one piece. The paper is first folded, inside facing up in the form of a Union Jack, steps (3) and (4). A flat octagon is produced when the diagonal lines are shortened to the length of the vertical and horizontal lines (5), that is, the lines formed by folding across the square (3). By folding each of the eight sides to the centre, (6) the base of the container is formed. The gusset is shaped by allowing the sides to fall to the centre (7) following the same direction all round, and pressing in place. If the folds are sharp the container can be opened, filled, and will then spring back into shape (8).

THE BOX

You will need:
Two squares of contrasting paper

To form its cubic space, the box has a square within the square, see plan (9). For size, the depth of the box measures half the length of the sides. Thus a square measuring 380 × 380 mm (15 × 15 in) will produce a box 75 mm (3 in) deep, and 150 mm (6 in) square.

Place the two papers together as for the octagon, and follow fold plan (9). The long red lines on the plan give folds back to form rectangles on the top of the completed box, revealing the lining paper. Stand the sides up from the base, folding in at the gusset, indicated as a short red line on the plan. Follow directions (10), forming the top, each piece locking over the piece in front.

41

Paper Cookery

Paper is used in cookery in many ways, and has been for centuries. It acts as an insulator against direct heat rays, spreading the heat evenly throughout the cooking process and preventing the food burning. Grease-proof paper is placed over large joints and poultry; brown paper is used to line the tins of heavy fruit cakes, cooked long and slowly. It is strong, grease- and water-proof. It is the cleanest of utensils, being used once then thrown away, and it is also very cheap.

HERRINGS EN PAPILLOTE

You will need:
Grease-proof paper
Olive oil *or* Butter
Brush (for oil)
2 herrings
50 g (2 oz) butter
2 cloves of garlic
Herbs, oregano, basil, parsley
Half a lemon
Pinch of mustard
Black pepper, salt

To cook *en papillote* is to enclose food in an envelope of paper, with herbs and seasoning, and a little oil or butter. The food is completely sealed in its paper case,

1 Take a large sheet of paper and place fish on the lower half, leaving room for folding the edges.

2 Fold in the sides of the greased paper all round, creasing firmly and holding the corners.

3 Taking the bottom and side folds of the paper twist the corner tightly, sealing the bag.

4 Remove the food from the oven, and unseal the case releasing the aroma of the dish.

and retains all its juices. No pan is needed. The papillote is placed on a grid in a moderate oven, and remains intact to the moment of being served at table. Because no water is used, none of the valuable vitamins are dissipated. Using sea salt and freshly ground black pepper will also enhance the flavours.

Herrings or mackerel do equally well for this recipe. First clean the fish, then prepare a herb butter for the stuffing as follows. Mix together the softened butter, chopped garlic, and herbs, add salt, mustard, and freshly ground black pepper, and moisten with a little lemon juice. Take a piece of grease-proof paper large enough to take two fish when it is folded, and brush it with oil or butter. Stuff the herrings and place on the lower half of the paper (1), put a slice of lemon on each, and sprinkle generously with chopped parsley. Fold the top half of the paper over the fish and fold in the edges (2), twisting the corners to seal the packet (3). Place on a grid in the oven pre-heated to 350°F, and cook for 40 minutes. The food can be prepared in individual bags and served up to each person still enclosed. Open the bag (4), releasing the flavour and aroma of the dish.

Other fish, meat and root vegetables can be cooked by this method. Potatoes are delicious; scrub, clean, but do not peel them. If they are small use them whole, otherwise, halve or quarter them. Put them on the greased paper, generously sprinkle with chopped parsley and garlic, season and dot with small nuts of butter. Fold and seal them in the same way, and put them in an oven pre-heated to 400°F, and cook for 45 minutes.

Locking Shapes

TREE AND STAR

You will need:
Sheet of card
Craft knife
Scissors
Ruler
Coloured sticky paper
Thread

Measure and cut out two triangles 150 × 200 mm (6 × 8 in). Cover both sides of both triangles with sticky paper and trim off the edges. At this stage, if you wish to make the fir tree, cut the edges as shown. Draw a line in pencil from the tip of the tree to the centre of the base and mark off half way. Cut one piece from the base to the centre and the other from the top to the centre. The cuts you make need to be the same thickness as the card so that they slot on to each other easily.

To make the stars, decorate the card on one side with horizontal stripes, on the reverse with vertical stripes. Cut out two identical four-pointed stars. Measure and cut the slits as in the trees and slot together. The stars can be suspended by a thread attached to the centre of the shape with the slit on top.

1 Cut out triangles and cover with sticky paper. Measure and cut the slit, slot together.

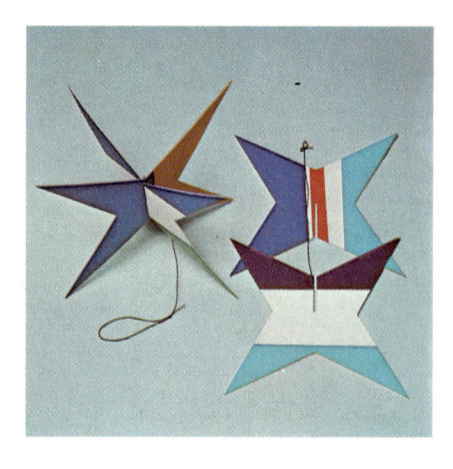

2 Decorate the card. Draw out and cut the stars. Cut the slit, and slot together. Hang.

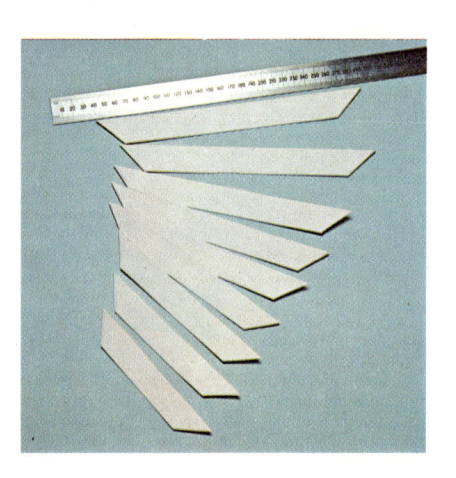

3 Measure and cut out all the strips and taper by 25 mm (1 in) at both ends.

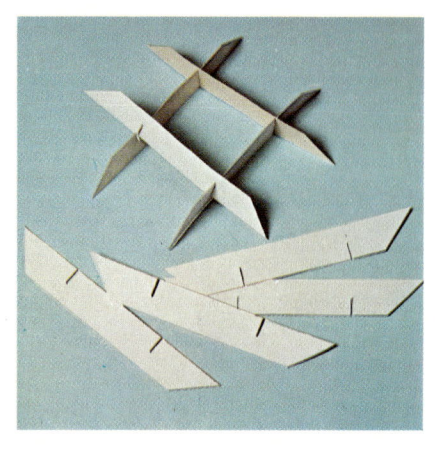

4 Cut 12 mm (½ in) deep slits in each group and slot each group of four together to form a square.

ILLUMINATED TREE

You will need:
1 × 1 m (1 × 1 yd) of card
Craft knife
Steel ruler
Felt pen, scissors, pencil

Cut the card into strips 25 mm (1 in) wide. Cut four lengths 300 mm (12 in) long. Cut the next four strips 12 mm (½ in) shorter and continue in this way until you reach 136 mm (5½ in). Starting with the longest strips measure 25 mm (1 in) and 50 mm (2 in) in from both ends of each strip, then taper the ends up to the first mark. Using the second mark, draw a line down the width of the strip and measure off half way. Take two from each group and cut up to the centre point from the bottom, then take the remaining two from each group and cut down from the top. Each group of four should lock together to form a square (4). Place the largest square down on a flat surface and position the next largest diagonally over it. Mark the points on the first square where the second one touches it, and cut 8 mm (⅜ in) slits. Slot the two squares together and place the third on top, parallel to the first; repeat the locking process. When all the squares are locked together, top the tree with two triangles locked together (6). If you have difficulty lining up the squares, cut a square 375 × 375 mm (15 × 15 in); draw lines on the diagonal and across it. Place your first square on the card, centre it, and stick it down with plastic adhesive. To make the structure permanent, glue the joints together. To illuminate the tree, insert a lamp-holder through one of the slats. Use only pigmy bulbs of about 15w.

5 Starting with the largest square, place the next one on top, and mark the junction.

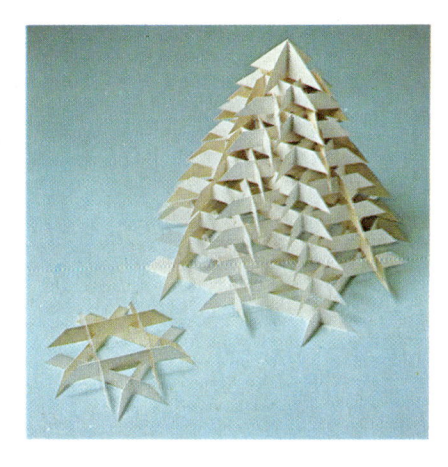

6 Cut the slits and join the squares together. Continue until all are joined. Top with triangles.

Boxed Boxes

You will need:
11 sheets of coloured paper
Steel ruler
Scissors

Select and arrange the eleven colours in order. Beginning with the top colour, cut out a square 150 × 150 mm (6 × 6 in). Using each colour in turn, cut a square 10 mm (½ in) smaller than the previous one, ending with a square 50 × 50 mm (2 × 2 in). Follow the folding instructions, making sure you get good, crisp folds. Each box when made should fit very neatly inside the last one.

To decorate the boxes, cut a square of paper the colour of the first box to decorate the second box, use the colour of the second box to decorate the third box, and continue in this way until you have decorated the smallest box; using the colour of the smallest box, decorate the largest box. A simple form of decoration employs the folding and cutting method (page 9). Fold a square of paper in half, and in half again, cutting snips out of the edges. When the square is opened out, it produces a snowflake pattern. Glue this to the outside bottom of

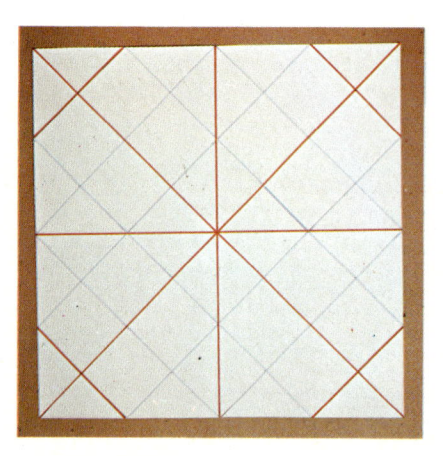

1 Lay paper white side up. Fold according to plan, blue folds in and red folds out.

2 Turn diagonally on, and fold two opposite corners in to the middle.

3 Using the next fold in, bring the sides up, making sharp, crisp folds.

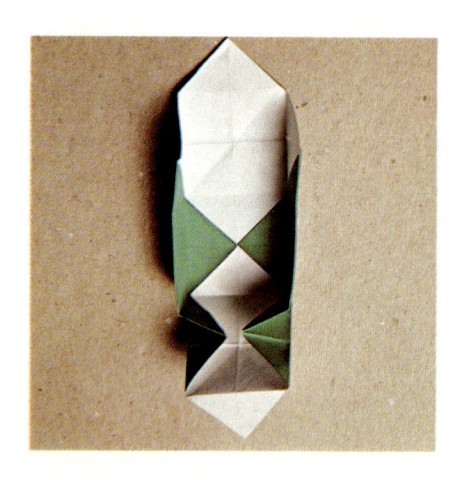

4 Fold in the corners to form the beginning of the third side of the box.

the box. Patterns can also be stuck to the sides.

These boxes are very quickly made and make fascinating presents, particularly if a small gift is placed in the little box, and the next box is put on as a lid. Turn that box over and put the next box on as a lid, and continue thus until all the boxes are put together. These boxes can be scaled up, but would need either to be made of stronger paper, or with a lining of paper or thin card. If scaled up, accommodate the extra thickness by doubling the difference, i.e., 10 mm (½ in), to 20 mm (1 in).

5 Bring the flap over, and tuck it down on to the base. Square off the angles by pinching the corners.

6 Repeat stages 4 and 5 to the other side of the box to finish. Straighten the sides.

47

Masks

A mask is a dramatic device for presenting a character or expressing an emotion — a new identity. A directional cut and fold in a piece of paper can create an immediate effect. Animals present different characteristics; strength, power, cunning. Study animals' heads, find the main structural lines, and use these as a base for the mask form. Use different papers, and add other curled and woven shapes to adapt the patterns here for other masks.

RABBIT

You will need:
Sheet of grey leather paper 600 × 275 mm (24 × 11 in)
Piece of violet paper
Two strips red paper, 600 × 50 mm (24 × 2 in)
Strips of black paper
Scrap of white paper
Scissors, glue

The rabbit mask is contained in a simple animal skull shape; it could be modified to make a sheep or a dog. The rabbit's characteristics are its ears and its teeth. Added embellishments are whiskers and a tongue. The mask, including headband, is cut in one

1 Fold paper, draw out mask, nose edge to fold. Assemble the pieces for tongue, whiskers and teeth.

2 Stick violet paper on back over eye position, cut lashes and poke forward.

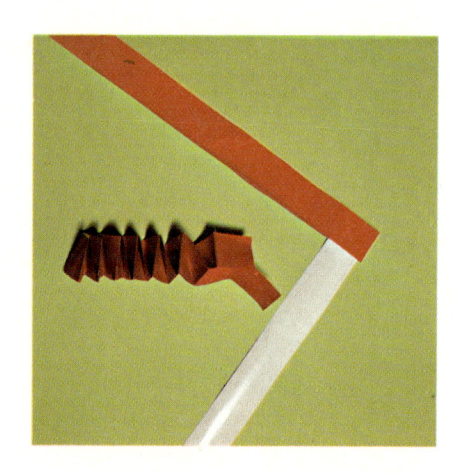

3 Cut strips for tongue. Join at right angles and weave by passing one over the other and folding back.

4 Slot in teeth and glue; stick tongue on to chin, and stick whiskers to cheek.

piece (1). From the nose-fold to the back measures 300 mm (12 in). Top of forehead to chin is 275 mm (11 in), from the centre of eye circle to fold is 55 mm (2¼ in), and the diameter of the eye is 35 mm (1⅜ in). Cut the whiskers from thin strips of black paper, split the ends and curl, making some rather floppy. The eyes are emphasized by sticking violet paper on the underside, giving a large, round, dark lashed expression (2). Cut and make forehead fold. Shape the jaw by cutting at either side of the tooth slot, join side pieces under to form jaw.

The ears are the two upper pieces on the pattern, overlapped and stuck, and the lower piece forms the headband. Try on for size before sticking. Make the tongue (3), and add the teeth.

EAGLE

You will need:
Gold paper 500 × 300 mm (20 × 12 in)
Red metallic paper 275 × 225 mm (11 × 9 in)
Strip of paper for headband

The eagle is a prepossessing character, with strong positive shapes. Draw out mask and cockade (5) and cut out. Cut on line across fold (5), and down fold 75 mm (3 in). The fold of the beak which creates the upper form should be calculated by the space needed to see through the eye slits; hold the mask to your face to gauge the distance before overlapping and sticking beak, and the area between the eyes (6). Lightly curl the gold strips and add the cockade (7), being careful when sticking it in to keep it above the eyeslits. Add a paper strip for the headband.

5 Mask is 300 mm (12 in) long, width to fold is 250 mm (10 in). Fold metallic paper for cockade.

6 Score round eyes, cut eye slits. Cut strips above eyes, and curl beak ends.

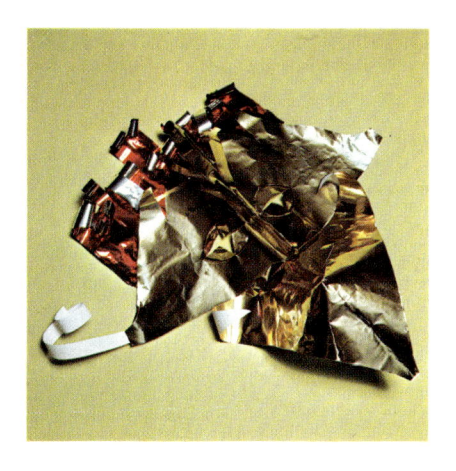

7 Cut strips in metallic paper and curl. Stick behind mask, after glueing between eye area.

Magic Theatre

THEATRE STRUCTURE

You will need:
Theatre casing — Strong cardboard for the base, 760 × 500 mm (30 × 20 in)
For the body — 2 sides, 500 × 450 mm (20 × 18 in)
Top, 550 × 420 mm (22 × 16½ in)
Back, 625 × 500 mm (25 × 20 in)
Wood or card for stiffeners of sides and top — 2 to each side, same length; 2 for the top, likewise
Black paper to cover all surfaces, inside and out; or black emulsion paint
Paint brush
Heavy black paper to make proscenium arch, 660 × 150 mm (26 × 6 in) for top and bottom, 600 × 150 mm (24 × 6 in) for each side
Rubber solution glue
Wood glue
Adhesive tape
Strong craft knife

The basic theatre structure is a collapsible box, which can be adapted to different purposes. It consists of a base, a hollow shell that fits over it with a removable back, and a proscenium arch in

1 Bend the sides of the cardboard through an angle of 90° to form the base.

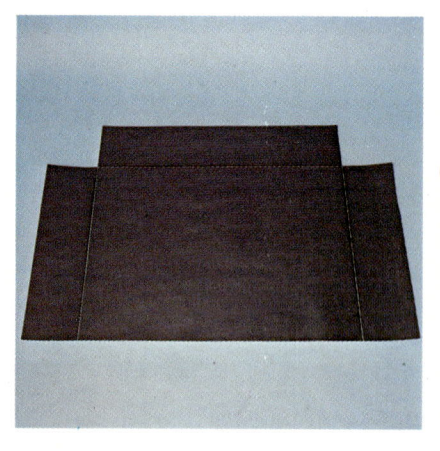

2 Cut two patterns, one slightly larger than the base, to cover inside and outside. Glue down.

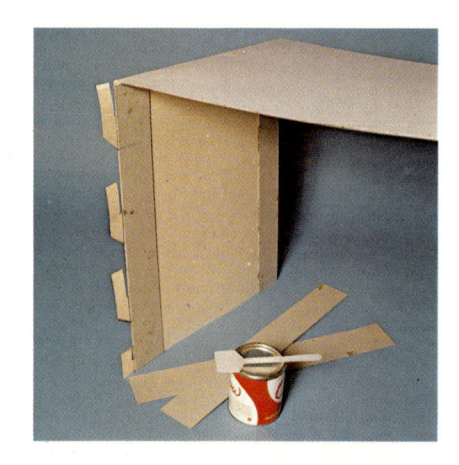

3 Glue stiffeners on inside of shell. Leave 3 mm (⅛ in) between top and sides to allow for bend.

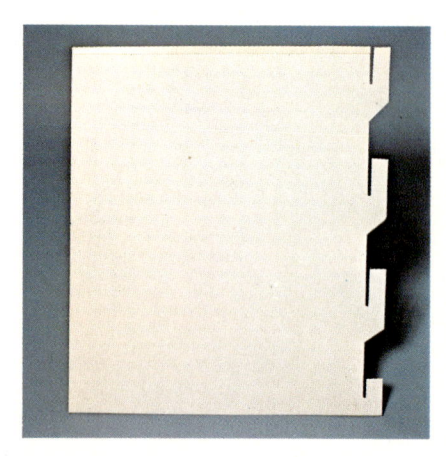

4 Measure teeth carefully, cut slots to take thickness of card, cut edges, both sides the same.

four pieces. The main parts should be of strong board, the proscenium arch of heavyweight paper. Because all attention will be focused on the inside, the box itself is black; if the cardboard is not black, it can easily be covered with paper, which will give additional strength; or painted with emulsion paint. It is advisable not to use too wet a paint, as this causes distortion in the card. The size of the box is arbitrary, but the measurements I have used give a good viewing area in a domestic setting. They can be scaled up or down in proportion. Start with the base, and take all subsequent measurements from there.

The Base

The base is an upturned lid, with one side missing. On the flat piece of cardboard for the base, draw a line 102 mm (4 in) within the edge on two short sides, and one long side. The inside shape forms the stage. With a scalpel, score along the lines for bending, as shown on page 26, and cut away the squares formed at the two corners by the overlapping lines. Turn the base over and bend up the sides, reinforcing on the inside with strong adhesive tape, and joining the corners with adhesive tape inside and out (1). Cover the base with the paper cut to shape (2) on the inside, and cover or paint the outside edges.

The Shell

To make the shell take the piece of card for the two sides and top. The sides are 500 mm (20 in) high, by 450 mm (18 in) deep; the top is 550 mm (22 in) across by 420 mm (16½ in) deep. The extra 40 mm (1½ in) depth on the sides is for the locking device to take the back. The shell is similar in form to the structure for the collage card base, see page 26,

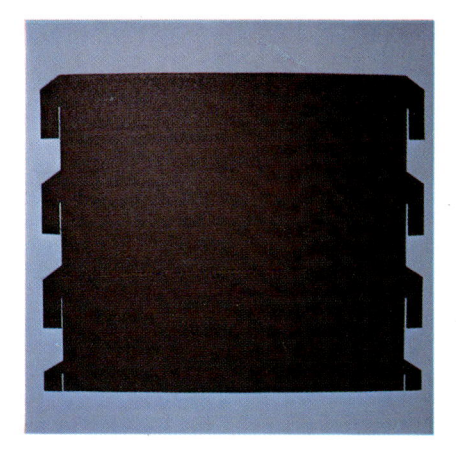

5 Match the back to the sides so that bottom of side slot meets top of back slot.

6 When locked in position, the back and sides will form a strong bond, and will remain rigid.

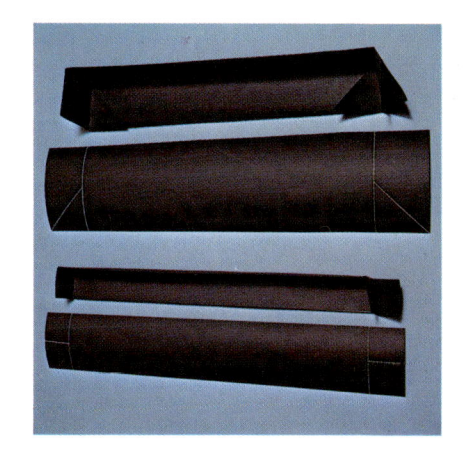

7 Fold proscenium pieces in half lengthways; cut and fold ends; glue to make corners.

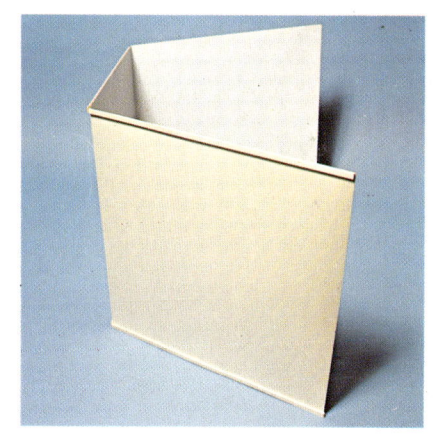

8 Score and fold set, with sides 400 mm (16 in), back 300 (12 in). Glue on stiffeners, top and bottom.

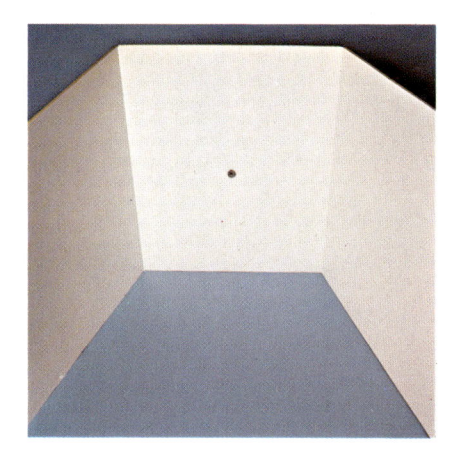

9 Make a hole in the centre back to take shaft. Glue washers on both sides.

10 Fit wood support at centre back, drill a hole through to locate shaft from back of set to back of box.

stood up on end. It is unlikely that one piece of card will be big enough for the whole structure, and you may have to join one or both sides with separate pieces. Do this by butting the two edges together, and using strong adhesive tape to join on the inside. Fold to a rightangle, and tape the outside join. The shell can now be stiffened, (3), using card, or thin fillets of wood. The stiffeners in the back edges of the sides should be 40 mm (1½ in) in, to coincide with the base measurement, leaving space for the locking device. The back is the same height as the sides, but wider to include the locking pattern, by 40 mm (1½ in) on each side. Steps 4 and 5 show the pattern to be cut. When making the device, clearance between the teeth must be allowed to set the back against the sides before slotting into place. The big locking teeth are each 100 mm (4 in) long with a slot 50 mm (2 in), and a space of 50 mm (2 in), finishing at the bottom with a 50 mm (2 in) with a 25 mm (1 in) slot. The teeth are cut away to make locking easier. The back follows the pattern of the sides, reversing the slot. To lock the back, place the shell face down, slot in the back, then place up in position on the base. The structure is now quite rigid (6). Cut the patterns for the proscenium arch (7) checking the outside measurements of the box and adjusting if necessary. Two alternative methods of cornering are shown, square or mitred. The square corner is a straight cut, one piece folded over the other to form a corner, lower picture on (7). To mitre, a cut is taken from the centre to the outside edge at an angle of 45°, the larger piece folded under onto the main part, the smaller folded to the corner, pictured at top of (7). These are

11 Glue small cylinders to the back of the discs and set the shaft in. Screw on grub screws tightly.

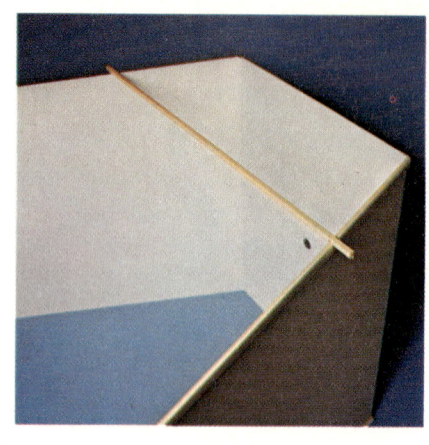

12 Notch the rod to fit onto the sides of the set at the top, a third of the way from the back.

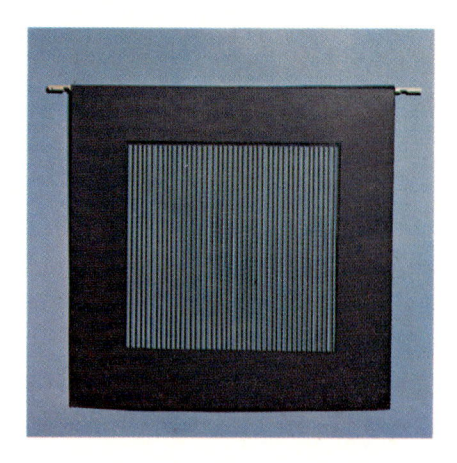

13 Cut acetate to size and apply black stripes. Make a black paper frame looping it over the rod.

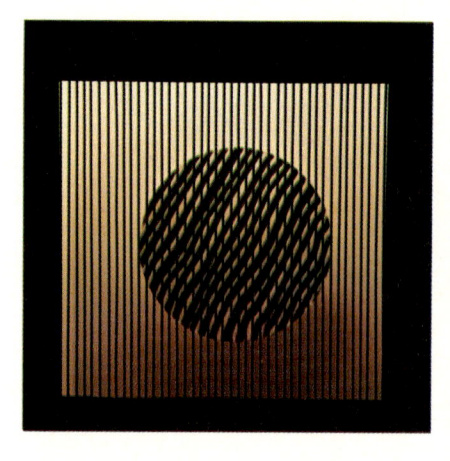

14 Effect in the box, carrying its own light source, either from a pigmy bulb or small battery.

15 Cut clear acetate to size, stick segments of coloured acetate on, and suspend from rod.

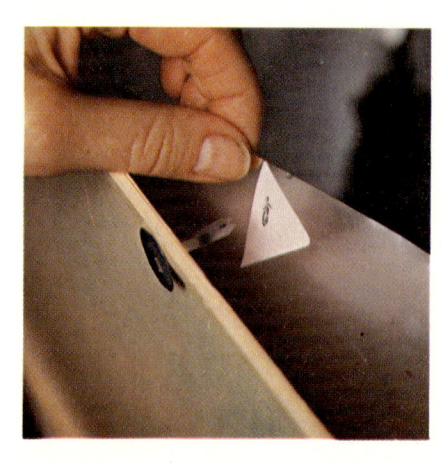

16 Cut slit and insert fasteners near front top on both sides of set. Attach foil. Open out fasteners.

now placed over sides, top, and bottom of the box. The box, covered in black, is now complete, like the box in the title picture but empty.

REVOLVING DISCS

You will need:
Inner set
Cardboard 1.2 m × 400 mm (44 × 16 in)
6 mm (¼ in) beading, to go full length top and bottom, for stiffening
Glue
Craft knife
Various patterned card discs, the diameter to be not greater than the back of the scene set
Thin metal shafts, about 90 mm (3½ in) long
Small cylinders with grub screw to fix shaft to disc
Wood for support 400 × 20 mm (16 × ¾ in)
6 metal washers, to pass shaft through back, set, and support
Fillets of wood, approx. 6 mm (¼ in) square, to hang across top of scene set, about 470 mm (18½ in) long
Acetate to make screens, clear and coloured
Black paper to frame screens
Optional: low-powered light to hang between disc and screen, mains or battery
Small motor, approx. 15 r.p.m.

The set is an inner skin, with sides sloping inward toward the back. This has the effect of focusing the visual field to the centre. The set is made in the same way as the shell, with stiffeners at the top and bottom on the outside of all three sections (8). A hole is made big enough to take the shaft of a disc. It is located at the centre, slightly above centre from the bottom (9). The washers prevent the hole from cracking. The wooden support carries the shaft through from the back of the set (10) through the back itself, where it can be attached to a motor, or hand operated.

Paint the disc patterns on thin card, and glue a small cylinder with grub screw to the back (11). Children's mechanical building toys very often have parts which are ideal for this purpose. Add a nylon or rubber washer to the shaft to prevent the disc catching on the back. Make a hole through the back of the theatre, lining it up to take the shaft and glueing washers on both sides of all holes. The disc can now be mounted. If a battery operated motor is used, this can be set up behind the back of the box at the right height. If the shaft from the motor is long enough, it can be passed through from the back and fitted to the disc. If not, attach the two shafts through a cylinder with two grub screws, screwing one on to the motor shaft and one on to the disc shaft.

The screens are made from acetate cut to fit in front of the disc, and hung from a rod which notches onto the top of the set (12 and 13). A small light can be hung similarly between the disc and the screen (14) carrying the flex through a hole in the back, or battery operated lights stood on the base. A moiré effect is created by a disc of black lines moving against a screen of black lines at rest. The coloured disc (15) will present a pattern of shapes appearing to jump backwards and forwards in space, as the colours change. Experiment with different combinations of colour and shapes.

REFLECTING MOBILE

You will need:
Mirror foil, to cover the base

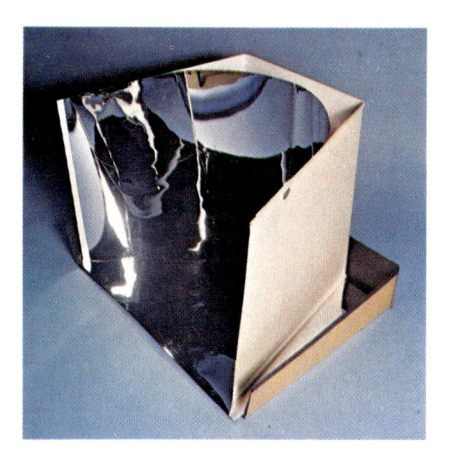

17 The foil will hang free, giving better images. The set can now be replaced in the box.

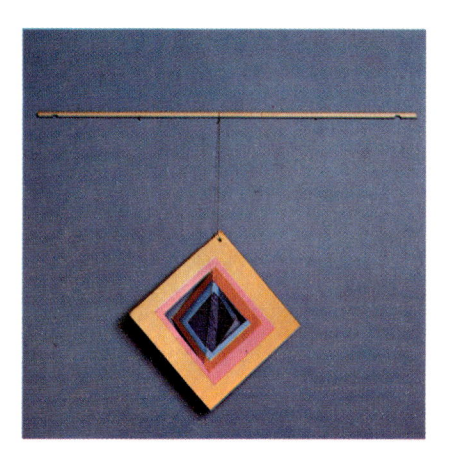

18 Suspend the mobile from the rod, and check for length, with room to hang freely.

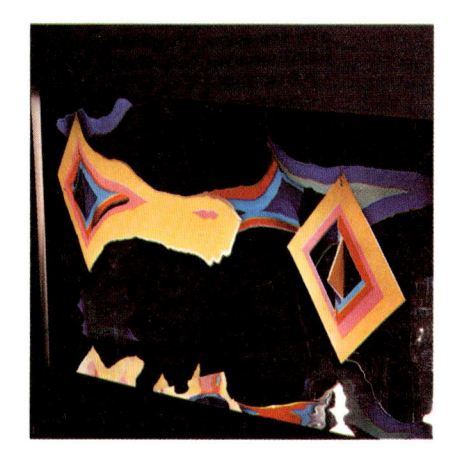

19 Hang the mobile in the set. Experiment with different outside light sources.

Mirror foil, the depth of the set and the length the sum of all three sides
2 metal paper fasteners
2 small pieces of gummed paper
A square of card, 150 × 150 mm (6 × 6 in)
Assorted coloured pieces of paper
Wooden rod to hang across set
Thread, to suspend mobile
Rubber solution glue

This mobile is very simple to make, and extremely effective. It presents ambiguous images which seem unrelated to the actual image, and confuses its position in space.

The mirror foil marks very easily, so handle it with care, and use a feather duster to remove surface dust. Cut a piece of foil the size of the theatre base, and leave it in place. Fix the paper fasteners to the set (16), and attach the mirror foil, backing the cut with a piece of gummed paper, and let it hang, forming a curve to the back (17). Place it in the theatre box. Make a simple and colourful mobile, using cut-out shapes, and coloured differently on each side; thread cotton through one corner and suspend from the rod (18). Several smaller mobiles can be suspended in the same way. Mirror-foil is a substance floated on a plastic base with a similar reflecting medium to silvered glass. Aluminium cooking foil will not give the same effect.

The theatre structure can be adapted as a Punch and Judy show for the papier maché puppets, see page 61.

Puppet Theatre

You will need:
The basic theatre box (minus the back)
Card for screen: 2 sides, 500 × 300 mm (20 × 12 in); front 550 × 500 mm (22 × 20 in)
Wood for stiffeners, approx. 5 × 15 mm (¼ × ¾ in), 2 to each side, and 2 for the top
Adhesive tape, or gummed paper
Rubber solution glue
Wood glue
Tracing paper or thin white paper, 550 × 500 mm (21½ × 20 in)
Strong craft knife
Electric light, about 60w power
Ruler

The puppet theatre is another activity that can be presented in the theatre box. Shadow puppetry is an entertainment that can give expression to imaginative and creative ideas; the puppet characters can be based on existing fantasies, plays and fairy tales; they can be abstract or figurative shapes derived from natural forms or mechanical parts; they can be naturalistic, or caricature, interpreting stories, or acting out specific incidents. They will be most effective co-ordinated with taped sound or music, chor-

1 Stick the paper carefully over the opening, stretching it slightly to make a taut screen.

2 Hold the puppets against the screen, keeping hands well behind the light source.

3 Cut parts ready for assembly. Pierce holes where wire joints and eyelets will be fitted.

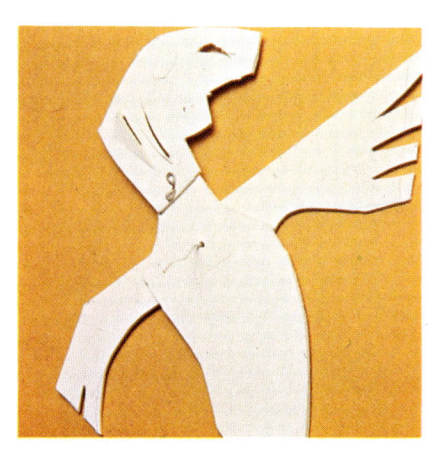

4 Make a figure of eight shape on end of wire, pass through holes, finish off with a figure-eight on other side.

55

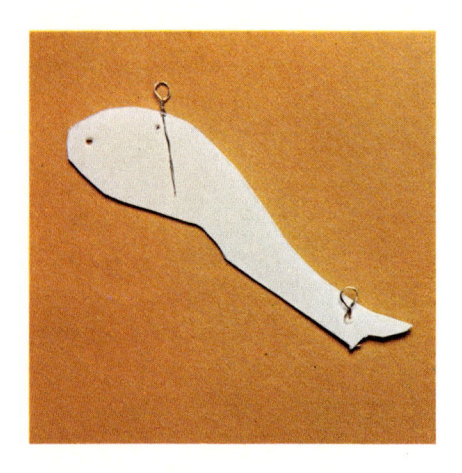

5 Make wire eyelets to take thread, pass through holes, finishing in a figure of eight.

6 Place flange of rod against back of puppet so that rod angles downwards, with eyelet on top.

7 Attach thread to eyelets on ankles, through thighs, and back through rod eyelet to puppeteer.

eographing their movements and rhythms, or creating an atmosphere. A festive game could be devised whereby short sequences are played through, scene by scene, leaving the audience to formulate a complete word or an activity, like dumb charades. For the theatre one needs a screen, that faces out toward the audience. This uses the method for the theatre set, but with the difference that the back is the front, and must completely fill the proscenium area.

Check the measurements from base to the top, and across the base. The wings must be long enough to support the structure, but will not be seen. Cut, score and bend the card, and reinforce the joints with adhesive tape, allowing hinge movements for easy storage.

To make the screen, cut an area from the middle section, which is in fact the front, leaving a border of about 40 mm (1½ in) all round. Cut a piece of tracing paper, or thin white paper, larger than the opening by 25 mm (1 in) all round, and stick to opening (1), using double-sided adhesive tape, or rubber solution glue. Apply stiffeners to top and bottom of the screen, structure all round. Place the theatre box on a table where there is plenty of room for movement behind, and take off the back. Keep proscenium arch in place so that structure will remain firm, and reverse the base, putting the open end at the back. Slide the screen snugly into the proscenium area, opening the wings out to the sides. Set a lamp in the base, beamed onto the screen (2), and the performance area is set. The intention is to illuminate as much of the screen area as possible, and the light should come between the screen and the manipulators of the puppets.

SHADOW PUPPETS

You will need:
A sheet of card
Thin dowelled rods, about 500 mm (20 in) long, one for each puppet
Panel pins
Eyelet rings, one for each rod
1 m (1 yd) strong thread
Small hammer
Adhesive tape
Glue
Floral or fuse wire
Wire cutters
Coloured acetate
Assorted ephemera, textured pieces
Strong craft knife
Gimlet

The puppets must be as flat as possible, the maximum shadow being obtained from parts pressed against the screen. They can be rigid, with parts stuck together; they can move arbitrarily, the parts wired loosely, their limbs flapping rhythmically depending on the rod movement; and they can be articulated, using threads to move the wired parts. Gather together pieces that will make interesting shadows, and using the card as a basis, make a pattern, allowing for overlap where parts are to be glued or wired (3). Line up the parts to be joined, and wire together (4). On head and wings, the wire can be fairly tight, enabling their position to be changed for each scene, and maintained. On the parts to be articulated, the wire should be loose enough to allow them to fall back into place. Fit eyelets to the top and bottom of both legs, on the side facing the puppeteer, towards the outside edge (5). Stick on all the decorative pieces.

Take the dowelled rod, and screw the small eyelet ring in, about 25 mm (1 in) from the end. Keeping the eyelet on top, cut the end at an angle, giving a downward slant from the puppet to its manipulator. Hold the puppet flat against the end, and hammer a small panel pin through; strengthen with adhesive tape (6). Take two lengths of thread, and tie to ankle eyelets, one on each leg. Thread as shown in (7), and pull gently to see if limbs are free. Make a mark, or use two differently coloured threads to distinguish left leg from right. By pulling gently on the thread, the legs will be raised; by releasing it, they will lower. Arms and other parts can be manipulated in this way, but too many threads become confusing and unmanageable. Finally, when making the puppets, relate their size to the size of the screen.

Simple silhouette puppets can be made by cutting single shapes out of thick black card. If you are not very good at drawing the outlines you can always trace your characters out of books or magazines and then transfer the traced image to the card. You can also 'set the scene' with cut out shapes of trees, houses, castles, stars and moons. These static shapes can be stuck to the inside of the screen with double sided adhesive and changed between scenes.

Below: The shadow puppet theatre in action seen from the front. The puppets must be kept close against the screen.

Papier Mâché

Papier maché is a very malleable medium, and has been used in many ways, particularly by the Japanese; much lacquered furniture, made of papier maché, was imported from Japan and China in the last century, and later made in this country. The most common articles seen are needlework tables, trays, and vases. It is strong and durable, and is not subject to movement in climatic changes, in the way that wood is.

HANGING BOWL

You will need:
Newspaper
Tissue paper
Scissors
Wallpaper paste
One plate
Three bowls
Ball
String

Papier maché is a very slow process, and you will need a full day in which to work. First decide the size the hanging bowl is to be, and find a similar sized ball. To prevent the ball from rolling around stand it on a collar, such as a roll of tape. Prepare all the paper first by cutting it into tri-

1 Soak some newspaper in water and coat the ball from the middle outwards.

2 Coat newspaper in glue-soaked tissue, coat that in glue-soaked newspaper. Repeat four times.

3 Allow to dry for at least a day, remove from the ball and trim the edges.

4 Paint inside and out with gloss paint. Thread the string through the rim in three places and hang.

5 Model the head from soft plasticine. Stick a tube in to form the neck. Place on a stand.

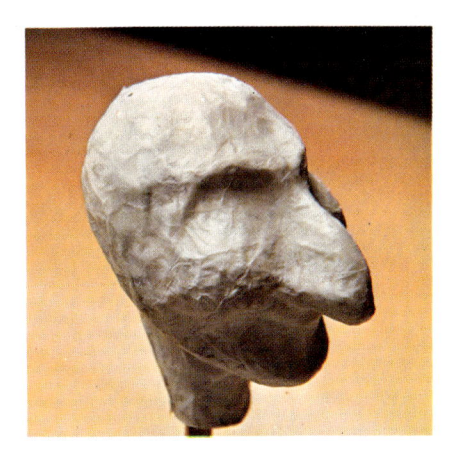

6 Using small strips of paper, coat with newspaper as in the previous exercise (1).

7 Draw a line round and carefully cut in half; remove plasticine and stick together again.

angles. Put the newspaper in one bowl, and the tissue into the other. Two different types of paper are necessary, so you can distinguish between layers as you work. Only use water on the first layer; this is important, for otherwise the completed bowl will be firmly stuck to the ball. The remaining layers need to be glue-soaked, the more layers built up the better. Allow plenty of time to dry.

GLOVE PUPPETS

Glove puppets are the easiest of the puppets to manipulate; all the animation is provided by the thumb and fingers. The index finger supports the head, and the thumb and middle finger, the arms. This means that the puppeteer can operate two puppets simultaneously. In fact, one person can operate a complete show, providing that not more than two characters are performing at any one time; though this makes demands on one's flexibility and vocal range. Some puppets also have legs. These are operated by the other hand, with the index finger and middle finger.

The most well-known of the glove puppet shows is Punch and Judy, a regular feature at fairs, parks and seaside resorts.

The origins of Punch are very ancient. He first appears in ancient Rome, where he is called a *Phersu;* he is next identified amongst the characters from the *Commedia dell'Arte*, in the sixteenth century; variously as Harlequin, Pulcinella, and even possibly Scaramouche; and the scenes performed by Punch, Judy and company probably stem from the *Commedia dell'Arte* repertoire, with additions from folklore.

PUNCH AND JUDY

You will need:
Newspaper
Tissue paper
Wallpaper paste
Scissors
Plasticine or modelling clay
Small sheet of card
One plate and two bowls
Coloured paper
Felt or fabric remnants
Glue
Paints
Varnish

First find a picture of Punch to help you with your modelling. Soften the plasticine in your hands for a while and then begin to model the face. Make all the features very exaggerated because, as each layer of paper is put on it softens down the features. When you are satisfied with your model, make up a tube of paper about 75 mm (3 in) long and wide enough to fit your index finger. Stick it firmly into the head to form the neck.

Tear the paper into long thin strips and soak the first layer in water. To avoid having to handle the head, stick a pencil into a lump of plasticine and stick the head on to that. Coat the head and part of the neck, (the lower part will be trimmed off later) with the water-soaked newspaper. Using the tissue paper next, soak it in paste and build up the second layer. Continue building up alternate layers of glue-soaked newspaper and tissue paper until you have done about eight layers. Leave to dry for at least a day; then cut in half, drawing a guide line first. Remove plasticine. Stick the two halves together again and cover the join with a few more bits of glue-soaked paper. Paint the face all

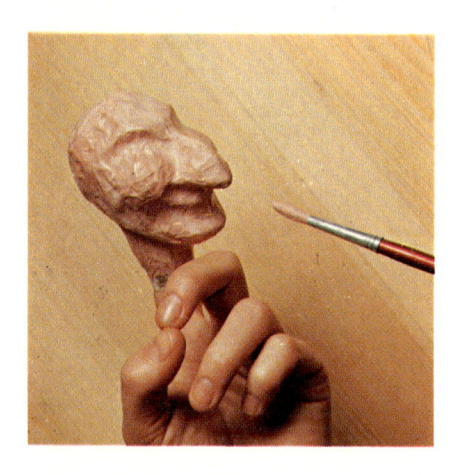

8 Cover join with glue-soaked tissue, leave to dry and paint all over in flesh-coloured paint.

9 When flesh colour is dry, paint the face in strong, exaggerated colours.

10 Cut strips of paper, snip all down one side and curl (page 8). Stick on from outside in to crown.

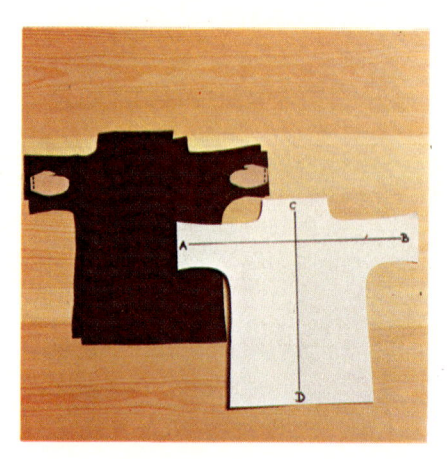

11 Make up the glove and hands; sew hands into the seam of the glove.

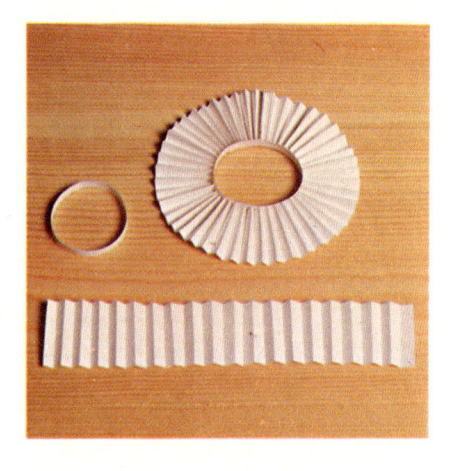

12 Make up the ruff from a long strip of pleated paper, and stick on to the glove.

13 Make the hat using the plan shown, and stick on to the head. Stick the head into the glove.

over in flesh coloured paint and leave to dry. Paint the features in exaggerated colours. Make the hair as shown, and stick it on, working from the outside in towards the crown. Make the hat either from paper or fabric and stick it on. Make a tube about 100 mm (4 in) long and stick it firmly right inside the neck, trim it off about 20 mm (¾ in) below the chin. Make the glove 230 mm (9¼ in) from A to B and 200 mm (8 in) from C to D. Place the hands facing inwards between the two layers with the thumbs upwards. Machine round, leaving the neck and base unstitched. Turn the glove the right way in, and stick on the ruff. Using a strong glue, stick the head into the glove.

This method of puppet-making can be adapted for other characters. Having made a Punch, you could make a Judy and the rest of the Punch family with a little modification and ingenuity. Then a Punch and Judy Show can be presented in its own theatre, by adapting the hollow shell of the theatre box and building a new proscenium arch. For this you will need brightly coloured sticky paper, and strong card. Use the method suggested in the theatre project, and attach a decorative, shaped top. Cover the facade with a bright base colour and stick stripes and patterns of a contrasting colour on top. The shell would need to be set on a hollow base, large enough for the puppeteers to operate in, this could be improvised with an arrangement of tables or chairs.

Scenery or back-drops could be made up of cardboard or canvas and painted very simply to add atmosphere to the show. Victorian street scenes are the most usual for Punch and Judy sets.

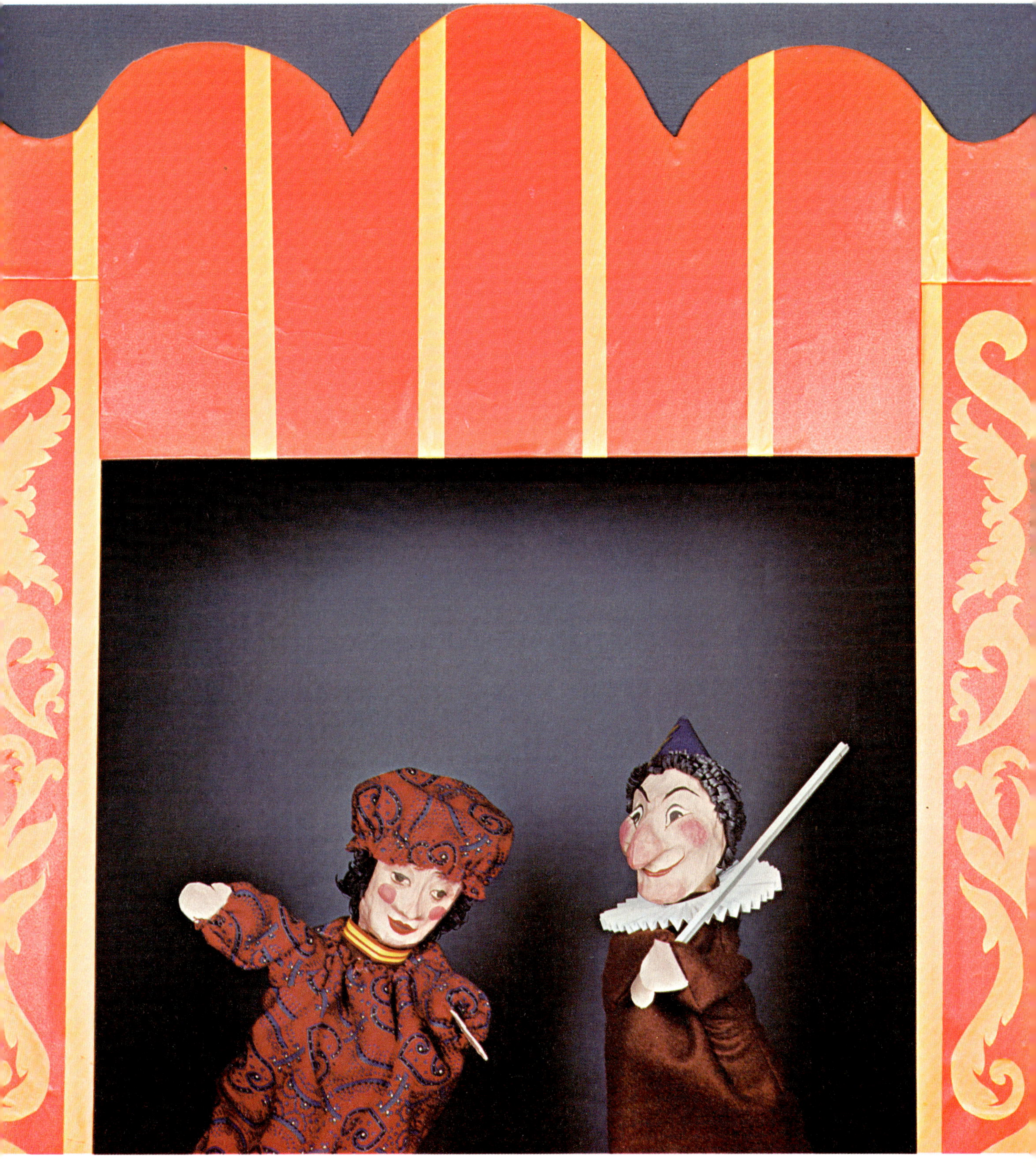

Kaleidoscope

You will need:
A cardboard tube, about 400 mm (16 in) long, 60 mm (2⅜ in) in diameter, open at one end
A tube about 100 mm (4 in) long, and slightly larger in diameter to fit over main tube
Card, 400 × 200 mm (16 × 8 in)
Mirror foil, 400 × 200 mm (16 × 8 in)
A piece of clear acetate, 150 mm (6 in) square
Strip of clear acetate 6 × 200mm (¼ × 8 in)
Pieces of coloured acetate
Piece of tracing paper
Paper to decorate the tube
Sheet of white drawing paper
Pencil
Compass
Ruler
Sharp craft knife
Glue
Transparent adhesive tape

The heart of the kaleidoscope is its mirror, providing variations of symmetrical patterns from the movements of coloured shapes. The hollow tube that holds it is closed at one end, with a small peephole in the centre, about 6 mm (¼ in) across. The mirror has three sides, facing inwards. They are almost the full length of the

1 The parts of the kaleidoscope. The main tube has one closed end, the outer tube is open both ends.

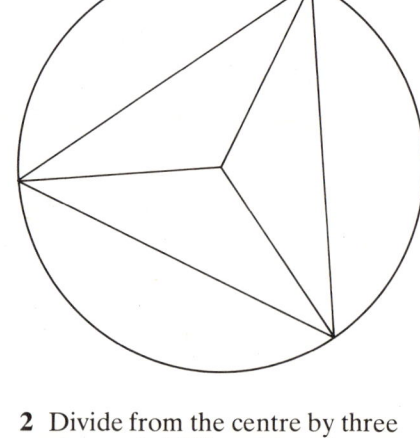

2 Divide from the centre by three angles, each 120°, and join the outer points on the circle.

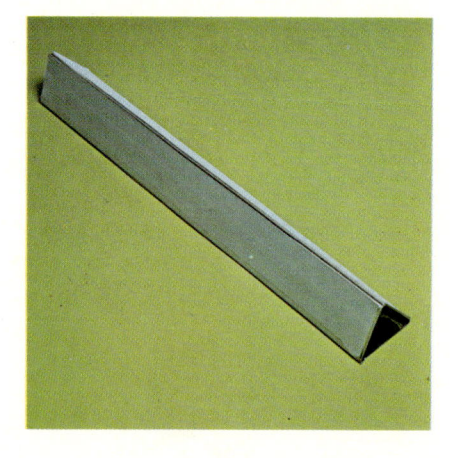

3 Score and bend the card, and join the third side with foil facing to the inside.

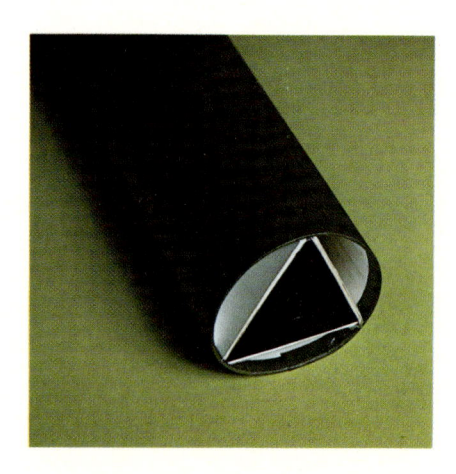

4 Fit the mirror into the tube, pushing it carefully right down to the end.

5 Cut two circles of acetate larger than diameter of tube, snip and fold edges to fit into tube.

6 Fit the sealed container into one end of the small tube, and stick in place checking the coloured chips.

7 Decorate the outside of the tube with coloured edging paper to finish it off.

tube (1). To find the width of the sides, draw a circle the inside diameter of the tube, and divide it as in (2). The lines drawn between the points on the circumference will give the measurement of the sides. Cut card and foil to the sum of the three sides by the length of the tube, and stick them together (3). Cut within the measurements, allowing the triangular mirror to slide into the tube (4). The patterns are made by coloured fragments moving in a sealed container. They can be made from translucent chips of acetate glass, or beads, that will move easily, and allow the light through, like the strips in (1). The container is made of clear acetate with a circle of tracing paper in the bottom (5), the inner diameter of the tube. The second circle is placed on top and a narrow strip of acetate stuck round the edge to seal the two parts together. It is now set into the outer tube, (6). When the whole tube is assembled (7), hold toward the light, and slowly revolve the outer tube.

The finished kaleidoscope can be decorated with collage or left plain. Make sure that the decoration does not make the tube too stiff to turn.